MW00415512

Jared,
Looking forward to
working together!
RJC

Together in the Cloud

The Ease and Convenience of Cloud Computing

Robert J. Chandler

www.RobertJChandler.com
www.togetherinthecloud.com

Creative
Team
Publishing

Creative Team Publishing
San Diego
www.CreativeTeamPublishing.com

Permissions and Credits:

Quotes from white paper and article written by Kacee Johnson, MBA, Vice President, Cloud service provider, © 2011 are used with permission.
 "How Cloud Computing Prevented Rain on Your Parade" published by CPA2Biz in their October, 2011 edition is quoted by permission of CPA-2Biz, (http://clientsolutions.cpa2biz.com).
Quotes from and references to Glen Aubrey, *Leadership Is—How to Build Your Legacy* © 2011 Glen Aubrey, and *L.E.A.D.—Learning, Education, Action, Destiny* © 2008 Glen Aubrey, published by Creative Team Publishing, are used by permission.
The online series entitled *Leadership Initiatives* article, "Recognizing and Seizing Opportunity" published by Creative Team Resources Group, Copyright 2010 is used by permission.

Disclaimer:

Together in the Cloud uses true stories to illustrate important points. Where permission to quote any story or a part of any story was not sought, the names and incidents have been completely altered. Any resemblance within these stories to any known entity, company, person, incident or issue, is purely coincidental.

ISBN: 978-0-9838919-9-4
PUBLISHED BY CREATIVE TEAM PUBLISHING
www.CreativeTeamPublishing.com
San Diego

Printed in the United States of America

Together in the Cloud

The Ease and Convenience of Cloud Computing

Robert J. Chandler

www.RobertJChandler.com
www.togetherinthecloud.com

The Cloud has forever altered how we store
and share information.
It improves the way we create, manage, and utilize data vital
to business and personal application.
The Cloud has changed our computing environment.

Some people resist change. Others embrace it.
Those who adapt to new methodologies learn that it's all about
using advanced technologies to help us become better at what
we do. It's all about creating and using tools that make positive
differences in other people's lives.

Welcome to the Cloud—part of your IT future from now on.

Foreword

Mark Wolgin, MD
Orthopaedic Surgeon

A Cloud User

What Is the Cloud and How Can It Help Me?

Simply stated, Cloud computing involves purchasing shared computer resources over a network instead of buying the computer hardware and requisite software.

My personal experience with the ease and convenience of Cloud computing involves interfaces that are both medical and personal. Our professional practice uses a web based electronic medical record system to which I have access from anywhere with an Internet connection, and which can be updated as needed as the medical environment changes. Our hospital also has a system to which I can log on from anywhere to enter orders or check information or images for any given patient. Personally, I use an online data service for document storage and email management, which makes my life manageable from anywhere.

While living in San Diego in 2006, and while exploring various options to expand computing power beyond the desktop, I was introduced to Robert Chandler who was using cloud technology to provide computing services to accountants. Recognizing Robert's clear intuition and leadership in this area, I added my voice to those encouraging him to write a book about his experiences and recommendations in this arena so that other business people could also access the efficiency and power of cloud computing for their business applications.

Whether they know it or not, most people these days are already participating in an environment of cloud computing. Examples of these very common activities which encompass electronic information transfers over a network include maintaining an online email account, participating with a social media website, banking or shopping online, or even following the directions to a location as outlined on a cell phone. Our interface with information technology (IT) on a daily basis continues to evolve, becoming more integrated in our lives.

Looking at the way we communicate and access information, some changes creep into our lives gradually, while others require more active involvement in the change. Choosing a new email account, posting a comment or photo on a social media site, or signing up to receive an electronic newsletter might not seem like a big change, and these are examples of relatively comfortable steps to take. However, for a business owner considering changing the information technology infrastructure of their company, with the potential to transfer much of their computing power and archives to an offsite location, there has to be a clear sense that the benefits outweigh the costs and risks before such a change is made. While the latter scenario is a much bigger step requiring careful planning, in many cases, businesses are finding compelling reasons to move their computing resources to the Cloud.

In these troubled economic times, business owners are continually looking for ways to become more efficient, provide services at lower cost, and give their customers access to their own information on a 24/7 basis in a secure setting.

To maintain the computing resources for a particular business on-site involves the need for a data center with servers in a temperature controlled environment, IT personnel (ideally with 24-hr. tech support) for intermittent software updates as needed, backup systems for data preservation, and constant vigilance to maintain information security. The costs to maintain on-site data services in each situation must be considered.

In a Cloud environment, however, these same computing functions can be provided at a lower cost with mirrored secure back up of data integrated into the system, and can incorporate a software infrastructure that can be updated as needed in a manner that is seamless and undetectable to the end user client.

As this book will show, Cloud computing, which is the wave of the future, can be applied to an unlimited range of situations now. Information can be archived. Applications and programs, which can be updated whenever necessary, are on computers in a shared data center. Cloud environments can be set up in a public or private manner, and end-users can collaborate on projects from anywhere with an Internet connection. All of the functions of the software of a desktop computer, along with other custom applications, can be accessed remotely, so a person doesn't have to be at their own computer to be productive.

Cloud computing is faster and costs less. The computing power is scalable so that the same applications could be used for many or a few users. Upgrades are taken care of automatically so security is maintained while the latest software versions can be available for use. Instead of buying servers and software, the end user pays only for the computing power that they need.

This book by Robert Chandler, a leader in his field, is an overview of cloud computing as it pertains to applications in the business world. If you have read up to this point, I would infer that the combination of your interest in the subject, along with the information contained in the following pages, will make your reading of this book a worthwhile endeavor.

Table of Contents

Dedication

This book is written especially for two groups of people who provide essential services to businesses. Their indispensible contributions help organizations run well. These two groups are Accountants and Business Owners.

Together these people set the standards of communication and effective business practices for their employees and customers. The methods they choose provide prime examples of vision and action that set the pace for success. When they work together in the Cloud there really are no limits as to what can be accomplished.

This book is also dedicated to my father, Ronald Chandler, who passed away in 2006. Dad, you were a great inspiration in my life and I thank you for everything that you taught me.

I also dedicate this book to my family, especially to my beautiful wife and daughter who have always believed in me and my dreams.

Together in the Cloud—
An Introduction

Business professionals and individuals are well acquainted with information technology (IT). They yearn for greater ease and convenience in their IT applications, as well as accuracy and security to help them get their jobs done better.

The Cloud assists them in many ways. Among them:

1. Sharing information: access anytime (readily available 24/7), anywhere (all that is needed is an Internet connection), in a multi-user environment (more than one person can access it) at the same time.

2. Creating and securely sending data files: so the people who should see them can access the information they need.

3. Remotely logging to a client's or staff member's computer: overcoming the challenges of multiple users at a single time, high security risks, slow speeds, and inconvenience.

4. Data backup (an automatic occurrence): assuring that information is accessible at any time.

5. Disaster recovery: data files are located offsite to assure ongoing accessibility.

6. Availability of software updates: helping you keep current.

7. Reducing the need to have an IT professional or IT consultant on staff: saving you money.

8. Instant access: business owners and accountants don't have to wait.

9. Keeping up with technological change: no need to spend hours searching for and researching solutions to common business data problems.

10. Work more efficiently: all it takes is an Internet connection.

Enter the Cloud. "Together in the Cloud" solves application, networking, appliances, server, and storage problems. The Cloud is a welcome addition to any business environment.

The Cloud is here to stay. Individuals and firms who embrace beneficial change adapt their methods, and experience increased opportunities for sustainable success. Never has this been truer than in creating, storing, accessing, and sharing information vital to business operations.

Fast (the speed of the transaction) can also be fine (the quality of the interaction) in new and rapidly developing IT environments. Efficiency and accuracy join hands in a globally ripe collection of economies and business practices where instant information sharing on accessible platforms is the new norm because it has to be.

Cooperation between people still is the standard of personal maturity, of course. But business growth depends on similar collaboration paradigms in "on demand" technological environments where requirements for immediate access to business information set new standards of engagement.

No more hesitation, tech inhibitors, unnecessary licensing hoops to jump through, and inconvenient (often hidden) next steps to take. No more dependence on unreliable IT consultants or on-site data storage systems where purchase and upgrading expenses mount quickly, guarantees are fragile if they exist at all, and retrieval of data is often far more complicated than it needs to be.

In Cloud computing, software, data, and operations literally are done online in a virtual office environment, one that is unencumbered by the hardware and software systems that have bogged down so many for so long. The Cloud has created an information processing *place*. The act of getting to the place of the Cloud has become a broader and higher standard of computing ease and efficiency. That place is where the needs of computing processes are fulfilled often beyond expectation. In the Cloud, sharing information within a secure environment has become not only possible—it's here.

Cloud computing energizes the user because it is uncomplicated and stress free. This fact sets it apart. Simplicity of use refreshes anyone who simply wants to get work done faster, more efficiently, and accurately without worrying about the hardware, security, software, and access issues.

So what is the Cloud? According to a white paper written in 2011 by Kacee Johnson, MBA, and Vice President of a Cloud service provider, "Cloud is used as a metaphor for the Internet. When you combine the 'Cloud' with 'Computing,' you get a virtualized IT infrastructure that is hosting your services and software online. One of the great benefits of Cloud Computing is that users don't need the knowledge of, expertise in, or control over the technology infrastructure that supports them. IT is being transformed to a utility based service rather than a traditional client-server infrastructure. Cloud Computing provides users with a highly scalable solution with resources and security that could not be replicated by a small-to-medium sized business owner. Providing common business applications online that are accessed via the Internet while the software and data are stored on servers at a remote data center, Cloud Computing has caused a shift in IT to be *on demand.* "

In the Cloud, users deal with their data in a real time and virtual environment. The Cloud is a single portal for multiple software applications, data storage, and retrieval. The bottom line for business users: ease and convenience are what being together is the Cloud is all about.

Users are moving away from traditional hardware and software IT platforms. They utilize the Internet to enhance performance of applications and systems they are already acquainted with. This move simply makes sense. It makes dollars and cents, too. Think of the convenience and cost savings of accessing IT operations anytime and anywhere where all that is needed is an Internet connection. And this technology is available to *any* industry.

Together in the Cloud is written to help businesses understand the possibilities of 21st Century computing methods utilizing present and future-encompassing technologies "in the Cloud." The book is designed to help you and those with whom you work to become more fulfilled personally and professionally because work is done more efficiently and profitably.

Join the expanding group of users who function better with this new technology. They use the Cloud as a tool of optimum security, operational efficiency, and enhanced productivity. They use it because it works.

These people are the ones who understand and enjoy the ease and convenience of Cloud computing. It was worth their time and effort to investigate and adapt to this new technology, and it's worth yours, too.

Come together in the Cloud. Here you can see clearly how computing in a virtual environment can enhance your personal and business success. After all, since we have to work, shouldn't work be made as easy as possible?

Glossary

At the outset let's define some of the words of Cloud Technology. Industries possess their own language, and computing in the Cloud is no exception.

Applications: a group of software programs installed on servers, designed for end users.

ASP: Application Service Provider.

Biometric Hand Scan: the authentication of humans through their hand print and fingerprints to garner access levels.

Byte: a unit of digital information or data.

Cloud: used as a metaphor for the Internet, a web-based environment for computing. The Cloud is the means of delivery for computing as a service rather than as a product whereby resources, software, applications, and information are provided to computers and other devices as a utility over a network.

CRM (Customer Relationship Manager): a method for managing a company's interactions with customers, clients and sales prospects, used to organize activities.

Data Center: An operations center that provides space, security, electricity, Internet connectivity, and engineering to oversee the Network Operations Center (NOC).

Disaster Recovery Plan: the process, policies and procedures for recovery or continuation of technology infrastructure after a natural or human caused disaster, to ensure business operations' continuity.

DMS (Document Management and Storage): a computer system (or set of computer programs) used to track and store electronic documents and/or images of paper documents.

Encryption: transforming data through an algorithm to ensure it is unreadable to anyone trying to "hack" into the layer of transport.

Exchange: collaborative applications which allow synchronization of email, calendar, and contacts.

Fail-over Plan: part of a disaster recovery plan that provides a backup server when another server fails.

GB (Gigabyte): a multiple unit of a byte (10^9)

Hands on Service: physical human beings on site for security and/or technical engineering.

Hybrid: infrastructure with two or more cloud types such as private, public, or dedicated.

IaaS (Infrastructure as a Service): a platform for virtualized servers on which users can install applications

ISP (Internet Service Provider): an organization that provides access to the Internet.

IT (Information Technology): the management of technology which includes but is not limited to computer software, applications, information systems, computer hardware, program languages, and data constructs.

KB (Kilobyte): a multiple unit of a byte (10^3)

Man Trap: a physical security system designed to entrap a person who has gained unauthorized access or to sound an alarm if a breach of security processes has occurred.

MSP (Managed Service Provider): the practice of transferring day-to-day related management responsibility utilizing a strategic method for improved, effective, and efficient operations including Production Support and lifecycle build/maintenance activities.

MB (Megabyte): a multiple unit of a byte (10^6)

MW (Megawatt): one million watts of power.

N+1/2N: forms of resilience to ensure system availability in the event of failure, N+1 will have one independent backup, and 2N refers to an uninterruptible power supply.

Network: the collection of hardware components interconnected/linked by communication channels.

NOC (Network Operations Center): one or more system monitoring locations from which control is exercised over a computer and network.

PB (Petabyte): a multiple unit of a byte (10^15)

PaaS (Platform as a Service): also known as Provision Hosting or Application Software Provider. This service provides the virtualization of servers, networks, and storage in the Cloud.

Private Cloud: An infrastructure operated for a single organization.

Proprietary Software: software that is licensed under exclusive rights by a company for their own use.

Public Cloud: A shared resource pool for users of multiple organizations utilizing the same applications.

RAID (Redundant Array of Independent Disks): a storage technology that combines multiple disk drive components into a logical unit. Data is distributed across the drives in one of several ways called "RAID levels" depending on what level of redundancy and performance (via parallel communication) is required.

RDP (Remote Desktop Protocol): a proprietary protocol that gives users a graphical interface to another machine.

Redundancy: multiple means of execution in that the system or server can be executed through several different components or layers to ensure that if one fails there is a backup plan.

SAS70 Type II: a statement of auditing standards performed by a 3rd party accrediting agency to ensure that proper standards are met.

Seamless Windows: provision of compatible and reverse usage for multiple monitors in a remote desktop environment.

Shared Environment: also known of as a "Public Cloud" where users from multiple organizations work on a server across multiple machines, sharing resources and common applications.

SLA (Service Level Agreement): a part of a service contract where the level of service is defined.

SaaS (Software as a Service): also referred to as "on-demand software," a software delivery model in which software and its associated data are hosted.

Storage: data repository that can be accessed by devices, where data is held in an electromagnetic or optical environment.

Tablet: a mobile computer larger than a phone, integrated with applications and the Internet.

TB (Terabyte): a multiple unit of a byte (10^{12})

TS (Terminal Server): network-accessed servers that allow organizations to connect multiple devices to a shared network.

TWAIN Compliant: hardware that is compliant with the image capture API (Application Programming Interface) for common operating systems, a standard used as an interface between image processing software and the hardware component.

Virtual: the creation of an image of a server rather than a physical host that is part of enterprise IT that can manage itself for utility computing.

Virtual Server: a method of delivery of virtual machines for high scalability and low cost on hardware and software components.

1

The New Business-Progressive

Technology helping business has come a long way. When I look back at my career, I see a growing trend of utilizing technology to the fullest. I also observe that some businesses have been reticent to embrace positive change. Those that have embraced it have made business operations far easier.

It was 1991. I was a District Manager for the largest Southern California newspaper and I worked in the Circulation Department for the publishing company. My job was to oversee the daily delivery of 2,500 newspapers which were delivered to home subscribers by newspaper carriers.

I recall growing up that about 90% of homes received their news through a newspaper everyday in my town. The paper was delivered in the morning, the afternoon, or sometimes both. My job was to make sure the news carriers delivered the newspaper by 5:00 P.M. Monday through Saturday and by 7:00 A.M. on Sunday to our home subscribers.

I remember always having to look for and find a local pay phone after 4:00 P.M. each day, and doing this every twenty minutes. Why did I need to find a pay phone? Because it was my responsibility to check in at the office for customer calls that had come in. Most of the calls or complaints the paper received before 5:00 P.M. concerned newspaper carriers who were short the number of newspapers they needed for their routes. The calls after 5:00 P.M. usually were complaints from customers who did not receive their newspaper or the paper they did receive was missing some type of insert, like the Sunday morning comics or the store coupons.

When I add up the time it would take me to find the pay phone, get out of my delivery truck, make the call, and get back into the delivery truck, it was time wasted. When pay phones were the only options, time and progress simply stood still.

Then later that year came the suit case mobile phone (I remember it as the bag phone). I got excited because I knew this would make my life so much easier. Why would a simple mobile device like this make my life easier? Well, there was no more frustration trying to find a store, market, or restaurant that had a pay phone that worked, or was not already tied up.

I now could call into the office from the comfort of my delivery truck and stay dry (even though it did not rain a lot in San Diego) and for those newspaper carriers who needed help, I was at their location within seconds or minutes after their call had come right to me. With this simple addition to my life, my job became automated, more productive, and my efficiency increased by at least 35%. I felt like I was more profitable to myself and my company.

A few years later our distribution of newspapers became even more automated when we did not even need to call into the office. By this time I was carrying a pager where messages and tasks were texted to me and I only needed to use the phone for emergency messages.

Technology changed our operations. Indeed, technology has changed our lives. Progressing from telephones to computers and smart phones, just think about what we can do with our cell phones now: send and receive calls, text messages, email, access the Internet, and use literally thousands of apps. It's like we can track everything anytime, anywhere as long as we have that handy device. While it may be small, it has become a very large and convenient component of our lives.

Technology certainly made my work life easier in 1991. Today, it makes life easier for everyone who uses it. Where once we were tied to the office in a chair for ten hours a day, we are now unleashed from our desks and in constant touch via mobile devices and the Internet.

In terms of managing, storing, retrieving, and working with data, now we can experience the ease and convenience of Cloud computing. Twenty years after the pay phone sagas concluded, technology has made business life a lot easier. With Cloud computing we share information "together." Clearly, this is an improvement.

Businesses that want to grow recognize the need for staying abreast of technological advances. But knowledge about technology and how it can help is not enough. Businesses must embrace it. While they may recognize needs to design and implement new methodologies, and even hire professionals to provide improvements that are shown to benefit them over the long term, good intentions do not translate into improved results unless they act.

Opportunities for improvements are everywhere, in every industry. They are usually blatantly revealed when the exigencies of circumstances scream that there must be better ways to get a job done! They push people to see problems and then consider whether or not they will continue to live within their difficulties, or do something about solving them.

Too many businesses enter and get stuck in what I call "risk consideration mode." While there is nothing wrong with recognizing and weighing risk, it is wrong to let risk rule the lack of any progress whatsoever. Businesses should look carefully at their problems and, depending on their levels of frustration, choose to venture down paths of improvement by changing their paradigm of thought and action, to embrace new technology and its beneficial results.

The issue here usually doesn't rest upon whether a solution can be designed or found with the technologies we have access to. The issue usually entails a consideration of whether the problem is perceived to be big enough to embrace necessary change in thought and action, and whether desire evolves into setting goals, acting upon them, and accomplishing the desired results.

"Doing it the way we always have" is the enemy of innovation and business-progressive thinking and acting. Times change, and people must adapt if they are to succeed. Technology forces people to consider altering their behaviors in line with improvements, or remain stagnant.

Even though the methods "we've always used" may have worked to this point (I mean, the pay phone was good for its day), when new and improved ways of operation are shown to be more effective, cost-saving, and production-enhancing, why wouldn't a business or an individual consider them and, having weighed them carefully, implement what they know to be prudent and profit-producing *because they have seen the benefits in the design and implementation?*

The answer to *that* question is the one that upon which enterprises rise or fall. You should consider this question and your answer to it especially if you are the leader of your enterprise.

You should consider this question as vital to living and working in the New Business-Progressive.

> Even though the methods "we've always used" may have worked to this point, when new and improved ways of operation are shown to be more effective, cost-saving, and production-enhancing, why wouldn't a business or an individual consider them and, having weighed them carefully, implement what they know to be prudent and profit-producing *because they have seen the benefits in the design and implementation?*

Technology can be friend or foe, of course, depending on how it's used. Technology is amoral. It has no inherent "good" or "bad" qualities. The technology user is the sole determiner of application and motive, success or failure, profit or loss, benefit or detriment.

Emotions can run high when a new idea is presented, especially if the idea is anchored to a rock solid ideal that benefits all involved. Emotions should not be the basis of making the decision, of course; rather, they are the positive feelings that inventors experience when they produce a solution that will benefit everyone involved.

The problem is not the dream, the motivation, or the proof

that any great idea will work. The problem is whether an individual or company wants the solution enough to make it happen because they see its proven benefits. If they want the positive results badly enough they change their behaviors; if they don't, they remain stuck where they are. It really is as simple as that.

Businesses today are challenged to reinvent themselves and their methods of operation on a consistent basis. It is not uncommon for aggressive, forward-thinking and acting companies to conduct reinvention practices every three years or less. Technological advances in systems, such as IT, often force more frequent adjustments. These adjustments become welcome changes in fast paced and highly competitive global business environments.

Those who want to survive and thrive realize that gear-shifting activities are parts of everyday business considerations. Staying on the cutting edge is not a static activity; it is highly dynamic. It requires a look at the past to treasure or correct what they've had, as well as a present day focus on accompanying activities to implement the changes they deem to be profitable (and that produce profit), developing perspectives that look to the future, that refuse to wait for things to change.

These perspectives and the people who share them embrace and employ positive change to produce better results that unbiased research has shown to be true, right, and beneficial.

Resistance to positive change usually originates from several negative sources. Among them: fear, laziness, dwelling in comfort zones, entrenched and immovable attitudes, selfishness, isolationism, protectionism, hidden agendas, and power-hungry positions that are easily threatened by anything that smacks of success that didn't come from the people in power. The bottom line: *insecurity* dwells and dramatizes its presence when all-out resistance to positive change is practiced. When you see it, you'll know.

Conversely, *security* dwells in proactive change, taking the initiative to positively alter behaviors when it is clearly shown that benefits will result.

Change comes whether or not businesses want it or like it. The only thing that doesn't change is the fact that change occurs.

One of the most aggressive and world-altering environments that change affects every day, is IT. In every industry, information technology is employed to enhance and improve human productivity.

Consider how IT has changed *your* life and impacted *your* environment over the last twenty years, over the last twenty months, over the last twenty weeks, over the last two days. Examples: microchips, cellular technology, tablets, smart phones, virtual offices, and the Cloud—all have altered the way information is communicated, choices are made, and computing is done. You can (and probably should) add to your list.

But the list alone will not change you or your business. Applying what's on the list, will.

2

The Story and Possibilities of Cloud Computing

According to common knowledge, it began as early as the 1960's. Its originator is believed to be John McCarthy, the man who coined the term, "artificial intelligence." He was the one who also stated that "computation may someday be organized as a public utility." While the roots of computing together in the Cloud can even be traced back to the 1950's and the ideas of Herb Grosch, the concept was more thoroughly explored by Douglas Parkhill in his book, *The Challenge of the Computer Utility* in 1966. While forms of cloud computing have expanded and exceeded original concepts, the basic premise has remained the same: do your computing "in the Cloud" because it's easy and convenient.

One interesting and provocative aspect is the Cloud's widening use with no end in sight as to the possibilities. Realistically, the question could be asked, "What *can't* be done 'in the Cloud?'"

Regardless of the size and complexity of a business, or considering individuals who simply want to grow and go with the times, there may be no other realistic option *if* the rewards are shown to outmatch perceived and real risks. The Internet is a complex interweaving of advancing information technologies that have forever changed the methods of information storage, retrieval, computing, and sharing.

Cloud computing carries little mystery when one understands its basic premise. Confusion, if it exists, rests in the mastery of its potential through the understanding of its uses and the unmitigated scope of its means. No one need be in awe of the Cloud. It doesn't rule us; it's a tool for us.

So consider the benefits of working together in the Cloud. There are many.

Benefits of Working Together in the Cloud

One is ease of access. You've heard the expression: "You can't get there from here." So often that sentence has rung true when it came to storing, accessing, protecting, and sharing data without the knowledge base of a highly paid "IT scholar" or purported "computer expert."

Dependence on IT—and to some degree everyone is dependent on it—now no longer has to mean dependence on inefficient work or even guesswork from anyone who may pride themselves in "knowing more than you do." In fact, "together in the Cloud" may eliminate some unneeded vendors all together. Now "anytime, anywhere" is not just a dream or a phrase—it's a working reality.

Another benefit is reduced costs—a welcome result in a struggling or even a healthy economy. While it is still recommended that business should purchase new computers every three years, buying associated software has been the bane of the professional and individual customers for a long time. One reason is the required expenditure of funds to "keep up with new technology." Acquiring the latest has often been more of a burden than a blessing.

Implementation in the Cloud simply doesn't require a continual outlay of cash for the purchase of software or even hardware. In fact, if done correctly, Cloud computing *reduces* hardware (servers) and software (downloaded programs) expenses, as well as cost factors associated with network management. Further, in some situations a customer pays only for what the customer uses according to the customer's need. Bottom line: an entity can save money—not to mention eliminating a lot of frustration—by working together in the Cloud.

Ease of implementation is another plus. Simply, with an Internet connection, the possibilities of getting started and becoming even more productive are easy and convenient. Who can put a value on easing concerns about the "how to" of using technology, especially for those who may be technologically "challenged"? The simple truth is that most people know about the Internet and can access it. For them (and that would be the vast majority) Cloud computing simply makes sense.

Storage of information is an additional benefit. There is only so much information that a local storage system can hold. With the Cloud, organizations and individuals can store significantly more data than on private computer systems. Further, there is no limit on the amount of bytes that can be archived as Internet storage systems continue to expand.

In the Cloud, servers are networked together. The number of servers (data centers) required by a company often depends on its size and the complexities of its organization, but there really are no "walls" here: larger organizations simply utilize more resources.

Automation is not a new term any more. In fact the expression was coined in 1912. It basically describes the technique of making something run automatically, that is, without continual human interface. Human labors—punching a button, pulling a crank, applying a substance, moving a load, repetitive jobs—have been replaced with machinery or mechanisms that once activated, perform the tasks for you.

Apply *automation* to working together in the Cloud. No longer do IT personnel (often well-paid professionals) need to worry about keeping their software up to date, or continually chasing down solutions to problems related to maintenance and efficient means of delivery of information. It's automated and continually backed up, so these professionals can turn their attention to increasing efficiency instead of engaging in unproductive and time wasting efforts doing what automation can do.

One of the related pluses to this is the reduced if not eliminated need to purchase additional servers to store data. As noted above, paying the expenses to technologically "keep up with the Jones's," is a thing of the past. The Cloud solves this; your additional servers are "there," but not at your office, and they are no longer your concern.

Businesses grow in stages. Their needs for IT grow incrementally, too. Therefore, one of the needs for every enterprise is the capability to grow technologically according to what a business needs, not as an outside vendor mandates. "Together in the Cloud" brings scalability home. Growth of the need for increased storage happens seamlessly and in the bite-sized chunks a business wants to take.

Instead of having to purchase expensive programs or hardware, a firm accesses what they need when they need it. *They* are in charge of scalability, allocation of resources, adapting to their particular circumstances. This represents freedom to the customer.

Realistically, companies can acquire what they need on a month-to-month basis, hourly, or even minute-to-minute without the requirements of purchasing expensive hardware that likely will become outdated over the next few weeks anyway. While software still needs to be purchased, updating it is automatic. Think of the convenience of incremental growth where two of the long lasting positive results are *not* overloading your servers or draining your cash!

Every business begins with a dream. The Cloud offers an even playing field where dreams can be realized through better choices of how money is expended. In short, small business can compete with big business if that is their desire, utilizing the same tools that Fortune 100 companies use.

Information technology may still compose a confusing conundrum for some. Working together in the Cloud helps alleviate many of these concerns. Just like the driver of a car who wants to travel to a destination but doesn't need to know *exactly* how the engine of the vehicle works, a consumer benefits from the knowledge of a skilled "mechanic" to manage possibilities and production of working in the Cloud.

Choosing a skilled vendor to help you with Cloud computing and hosting may not be an option, especially as a business grows. Finding the right Cloud vendor is important. Often customers need guidelines to help them make the right choice.

Several factors emerge.

- One is reliability. An experienced vendor with a proven history of quality performance, positive reputation, up-to-date certifications, and stellar client relations seen in customer testimonials, is sure to be better than hiring numerous IT staff with varying levels of experience and perhaps unknown accountability and trustworthiness.

- Another factor is accessibility. How often and quickly can you reach your IT vendor? Closed for the weekend, out to lunch, away for the holidays? How about 24/7/365 accessibility "anytime, anywhere"? Help desk support is vital to a business that can't wait for the answers to pressing issues.

- Yet another consideration is pricing—this vendor should save you money. Part of their Service Level Agreement (SLA) should detail exactly what you will receive for the money you pay.

- Choose a vendor you can trust, one with experience that you can contact at a moment's notice. Speed here is no longer optional; it's required. The need for data doesn't wait. (See Chapter 10, Vendor Checklist.)

Closely related to automation is the need for automatic updates. The speed at which technology moves and improves is virtually incomprehensible. New ideas don't happen one at a time, of course. They come at amazing rates, often simultaneously. They are driving challenges and opportunities that only imagination and creativity can meet. And there is no limit to imagination and creativity.

Updates, when they occur, should happen without a user initiating or having to stimulate the process, or cajoling the vendor. They should simply "happen." Fortunately in the Cloud, they do. It's another worry gone for the people who use it.

I use the phrase, "anytime, anywhere" as have many others. The phrase has become commonplace, but unfortunately, its reality has not. Enter remote access. You are not at the office, nor are your accounting professionals, nor are your department managers. You are all at a convention in Las Vegas about Cloud computing and your software or hardware integrated systems back at home, go down. The guy you left in charge sees stuff on his computer screen that he has never seen before, utters a few choice epithets after he worries himself sick that he was the cause of the malady, then calls you. Now what?

Well, remote access in the Cloud can retrieve what the system at the office could not. The blessing is that you have already integrated together into the Cloud and your information is secure. The guy at the office is kind of off the hook, at least for now. But no longer is your data subject to the whims of strictly localized access or management. You know you have made a great choice when you chose to work together in the Cloud.

Your response time was virtually immediate, certainly faster in most cases than it would have been using a standard server and hardware. This is all about flexibility and ease, not rigidity and rules. Simply put, response time should not be subject to the inhibitions of older and tattered technology that prides itself in ruling the user.

Flexibility is freedom. It is freedom *from* road blocks and freedom *to* create new pathways of information sharing.

Mobility is another advantage. Tablets, smart phones, and other ingenious devices proclaim that you can take data acquisition anywhere. And you should be able to do this.

Being chained to a desk isn't practical and often not profitable. Go where you want, do what you need to do, because the technology in the Cloud allows you to perform in these ways.

So what of your IT staff or those employees who depend on them? Ask them how open they are to innovation, especially to working in the Cloud. Don't inquire *if* they are; inquire *how open* they are. Resistance usually comes from turf protection or insecurity. "What if technology replaces me and my position?" is often a verbalized or thought enhanced question.

Paul's Story

Paul was the original designer of his company's website. When first hired on in the mid-90's he felt secure in his position simply because he knew more than others who used the website, including its promotional features, email functions, and payment options for services and products. Many customers along with company staff benefited from it.

As technology advanced, however, Paul did not—or at least his reticence to grow and adapt became apparent as changes came along. Soon he was presented with opportunities for IT training and expansion of responsibility but his comfort zone didn't seem to accommodate meeting the company's technological require-ments, at least at first.

Paul lagged and then became threatened in his position when the demands of his department outstripped his desires for change. On the verge of becoming a casualty of progress by his own making, thankfully, he changed. He learned, adapted, and became even more valuable when the IT department staff grew and he became its leader.

Where would a company be in the short term (not to men-tion the long term if it wants to survive and thrive) if it *didn't* embrace technology and teach its IT and other staff people to do the same? The answer to that question will vary according to the health and vitality of the firm, of course, but the bottom line remains this: without technology-friendly use of innovation, a company's growth may stumble and slow down, or eventually halt, and the IT people and other staff could be out of a job regardless.

If you're the leader, engage your IT staff and company employees in exploring all that the Cloud can do for them and for you. Take charge here and open their eyes (because your eyes will have already been opened) to the possibilities of improvement in an ever expanding paradigm of qualitative choices.

Likely there is room and opportunity for everyone who wants to remain with a company when efficiency replaces the status quo *if* the people involved truly want to grow.

Likely there is room and opportunity for everyone who wants to remain with a company when efficiency replaces the status quo *if* the people involved truly want to grow.

Efficiency becomes paramount because it is freeing. Productivity replaces waste because it's the natural result of recognizing and implementing people's potential.

When combined, great attitudes and matching technology

create a no-limits environment for what can be accomplished. Staff personnel become empowered when they are not threatened by ignorance or incorrect information. When they know, they grow. Further, their productivity should cost less than the expenditures to engage them in this new paradigm.

Leaders take the lead in instituting new understandings and actions from fresh perspectives. Employees capture these views and adopt the changes that come from a leader's vision. In fact, there may not be any other suitable options than to see your employees as people who are more important than what they do, and because you see them this way, to help them do what they do, better.

Invest in them, teach them improved ways of operation, and show them how to become more valuable to themselves and to the company as they embrace new technology and learn how to use it. These kinds of changes can truly lift them to a higher level of worth and production.

Get them working together in the Cloud. When you do, your workers suddenly can access information quicker and provide improved solutions. IT staff are redirected to use their time more effectively and not waste your material resources. Customers of your company benefit too, because you and your staff become better at who are you and what you do.

Dealing with IT Staff

The Cloud will continue to have an impact on IT. In fact, it often shapes how IT is done.

In the new world of IT management, different solutions are required to address more "traditional" problems. Roles in IT change when confronted with the challenge of addressing lingering problems with better solutions.

A partial list of these challenges and changes includes:

- Security: older methods are being replaced with more secure "virtual" computing environments where encryption plays a vital role.

- "Share Ability": making information available to appropriate and authorized people speeds up the process of sharing data in real time.

- Ease of Use: not much more needs to be said on this one except, "It's easy to use."

- User Identity Management: only authorized people who have appropriate credentials and user identity can access information in the Cloud; it's easy to manage who has access to what. Identity management will need to be managed by a Single Sign On system that controls all of the users and applications all over the web.

- Backup strategy: processes of disaster recovery will change since key documents and data will not be on local servers.

- Infrastructure needs: local files, applications, and database servers will no longer be required to host office software.

- IT labor and HR issues: in this new environment a complete understanding and adherence by IT people to labor laws, company requirements, and diligence to perform them, are necessary.

In short, IT must alter its understanding, willingness, and work methods to meet a new set of demands in an ever expanding collection of business needs. Models of IT interface that were the methods of the day several years ago will not work well in this new environment.

Sometimes people who are the ones most heavily vested with innovation are the ones most resistant to change. In resistance they dwell in a place of power without understanding, and perhaps lack a desire to use their position well.

Your IT staff may have needs for job security as virtually all employees do. Perhaps you have seen this, or if IT personnel are particularly insecure, they may have even told you this, especially when it all "depends" on them for IT operations to function smoothly!

If this "need for coming to work tomorrow" means that information is hoarded, or access is difficult or denied to the people who need it, or dependence upon those who manage IT appears to be a prerequisite for normal business operations, then that need must be addressed and the processes of positive change started and implemented. If a need for job security becomes an excuse to not perform duty with diligence or somehow promotes staff to ignore labor laws, then these issues must be confronted head on. Technology should make jobs easier but faithfulness to a task and adherence to appropriate and lawful procedures must still occur.

One thing the Cloud does with appropriate safeguards is allow people who need access to information and who are authorized to obtain it, to get it without undue interference from company inhibitors, "brake pedal" mentalities, and the thwarting methods of so-called "gatekeepers" who mistakenly believe that *they* are the only portals through which all requests must pass.

Setting up and implementing Cloud services are easy for most everyone, about as easy as getting a free email address or joining a social networks page. Because of this simplicity, there are few, if any who have an interest in ease of efficient operation who cannot make this work.

Further, setting up and working together in the Cloud allows IT staff to literally "shift focus" from a reactive stance to a proactive stance. No longer do the IT professionals have to react to acquiring server updates and staying abreast of emerging computing issues; rather, these people can do what probably caused them to enter IT in the first place: concentrate on innovation and problem solving.

Secure data centers help relax nervous IT professionals when they know that the word *secure* is more than a sales mantra. They also experience relief when they don't have to enter the foreboding "Storage Closet" (server room) when the power goes down due to natural disasters such as hurricanes or earthquakes, or the human inhibitors of a construction worker inadvertently severing a power line to the server room. Oops.

IT staff members (and those that depend on them) are back at work as soon as an Internet connection is active. This is truly disaster relief, another huge benefit of working together in the Cloud. And for IT folks, this is freedom from unnecessary control and a new focus toward making greater contributions as part of a working team.

Creative Stimulation

Companies that are forward-thinking rely on innovation. They have to. In fact, if they are truly progressive, they make innovation a part of their strategic plan. Stifling innovation simply doesn't make sense. Releasing professionals from the doldrums of reactivity simply means they can concentrate on providing the professional labor they were hired to provide at the outset.

Working together in the Cloud allows the people who are talented in technology, to build and utilize whatever their imagination designs and a business entity truly desires. Cloud applications allow a business to select appropriate applications for their current needs at the time and that makes time and dollar sense for everyone.

It doesn't get much better than that in the broad perspective. This alone can release a lot of creativity into any company's daily routines.

3

Calming the Storm

Jane was an accountant who was hired by various professional organizations to perform confidential bookkeeping and accounting tasks. Her list of clients was growing as was her reputation as a dependable vendor.

One of her clients was a prestigious law firm. On the appointed day for her to be on-site she showed up to conduct her business. Completing her assignment she made a backup of the financial information on her thumb drive which included the accounting information of over 500 of the top attorneys in Los Angeles. She put the thumb drive in her purse.

Later that evening she decided to go see a movie. Before the feature presentation began she visited the restroom but forgot her purse, leaving it in her seat. When she returned she found that her purse was missing along with the thumb drive and all of the financial information stored on it.

How should she inform her attorney client of this huge security breach problem? This situation was going to be awkward at least, it could result in the loss of a major client, and might carry with it significant liability concerns.

If Jane had been using the Cloud, her accounting information would have been secure. The Cloud would not reside in her purse, of course, so her losses—the contents of a purse that could be replaced—would have been far less.

The Cloud Did Not Collapse

On September 8, 2011 virtually all of Southern California and parts of Arizona experienced a massive power blackout. It was caused by human error—an employee with the Arizona Public Service (APS), a utility company, was working on a capacitor at a substation near Yuma, Arizona, just across the California-Arizona border. This APS employee's error caused more than 8 million customers to be without power for several hours.

When the power goes out, the network shuts down, right? Well, not if you are using the Cloud. From an article entitled, "How Cloud Computing Prevented Rain on Your Parade", part of Transforming Client Accounting Blog, published by CPA2Biz (http://clientsolutions.cpa2biz.com) in their October, 2011 edition, quoted here by permission: "There was a two-week period less than a month ago when a hurricane, wildfire, earthquake and electrical blackout gave business owners and financial professionals something to think about—disaster recovery and cloud computing. How could they keep their business running, when events out of their control were happening around them?

"Millions of people were without power during those seemly one-on-top-of-the-other events, which could have put business at a standstill for many small business owners, accountants, and CPA firms." The article goes on to state that several accounting professionals leveraged Cloud-based solutions "…to prevent rain from falling on their clients' parade during these back-to-back events."

I was interviewed and quoted in this article. I stated, "More than 85% of our clients, which are CPA firms, could have been impacted by the power outage. It could have brought them to their knees. But with the Cloud, there wasn't even a blip on their radar screen. None of our clients experienced downtime during the power outage in Southern California. The Cloud did not collapse."

Uninterrupted Service

During the crisis, my firm maintained uninterrupted service for our clients. There were no failures. Here's why: our company's up to date data center provided our customers with high levels of redundancy to ensure that infrastructures services were always available.

Truthfully, the Cloud didn't collapse then and it can't collapse now because these redundancies are built in. If one server goes down, the others start up. My facility's generators, on-site fuel storage, and fuel supply contracts keep an uninterrupted power supply for an indefinite period of time. During the power outage in September of 2011, those provisions kept users up while much of the state was without power.

Certainly this kind of assurance breeds confidence. This confidence in technology promotes competence in continuing business applications. Customers can be assured that regardless of circumstances, data is safe as is their accessibility.

Storms come in life—some are real, others are manmade. Regardless of their sources, they are part of the course of business. Business is heavily dependent on technology. When storms and technology collide, a safe environment is necessary. Having and utilizing a secure environment to assure that vital data is safe and secure really isn't optional any more.

4

The Cloud and the Professional World
of Accounting

Numbers Have Moved to the Cloud

My experience is as an accounting professional. People in the profession greatly benefit from working together in the Cloud. I deal with accountants every day and provide Cloud services to them. We want these professionals to know the benefits available to them.

In this chapter I will address some specific applications regarding how the Cloud benefits people in my specific profession. The bottom line is this: the Cloud has changed the world of accounting. Numbers have moved to the Cloud. This concept is not new—it dates back to the early 1990's. Many accounting firms have started to take advantage of the online technology within the last few years.

Today's technology is used by more and more accounting professionals and business owners to accomplish their tasks with far more convenience and efficiency. These new methods provide mutual benefits as owners and accountants work together in the Cloud.

While most of the advantages have been around for some time, they are now finally being utilized as they should be. Consider four unique mutual benefits of online client accounting.

Ease of Access

Being online to conduct business is no longer a dream or a wish. It's a requirement professionally and personally. The most powerful feature and benefit of working in the Cloud is accessing information anytime, anywhere. All that is needed is an Internet connection.

We are all "wired" to the Internet. Ease of access means ease of storing, inputting, retrieving, and sharing accounting information. Online technology allows instantaneous access for authorized people to see where their business stands: reviewing financial statements, accounts payable and accounts receivable, along with access to documents, financial charts, and spreadsheets.

Compared to many cumbersome practices of the past, well, there really is no comparison. The Cloud has changed, and is continually improving the way accounting is conducted.

Sharing Information in Real Time

Ease of access naturally leads to enhanced capability of sharing information. Financial data can be accessed by business owners and their employees, staff, clients, shareholders, and consultants regardless of their physical location.

No one has to wait for the answers as economic issues arise (and they always do). The answers are available immediately and can be accessed by any authorized individual at any time.

Sharing information in this way enhances client and accounting relationships. Accountants become more valuable to their clients because the accountant can see how their client's business is performing without the client having to make the first move. These relationships are proactive, not reactive, empowering accountants to do what clients want them to do: help a business make good financial decisions and grow its bottom line.

Sharing information in the Cloud means that banking and accounting are done in real time. Wondering about, and waiting for information, are eliminated.

Use of an Application Service Provider (ASP) has become

popular because data is centralized in one place. "Centralized computing" saves companies thousands in technology infrastructure (no need to manage applications, files, email servers) and software costs.

A licensed vendor or host assures that the client and accountant have one central location to access information. To become an authorized and licensed host, an independent, outside party reviews and audits the security, privacy, availability, and financial integrity of the vendor.

If you are considering moving to the online accounting world, make sure you use a company that has up to date certifications from the vendors they use. These certifications help the client and the vendor know that data is secure, and that procedures are conducted correctly.

Most companies have started to take advantage of Cloud technology within the last several years. For those who use Cloud technology, desktop and laptop computers now have become "dummy terminals" because all that's needed is an Internet connection.

Redundancy

Another clear benefit is redundancy. Financial information is backed up in the Cloud.

Access to vital financial information is not dependent any longer on in-house computers and software that may (and eventually will) fail. Backup in multiple locations simply makes sense.

In the Cloud, the locations for storage are virtually limitless. Redundancy brings comfort to business owners who know that their information won't be lost.

Finally, the result of ease of access, sharing information, risk management, and redundancy, is recovery. You can get it back.

Disaster recovery—knowing that information will never be lost permanently—is the endgame benefit of online client accounting.

Every decision in business depends on timely and accurate information. When disasters strike, regardless of their causes, a business professional can be assured that if he and his accountant are working together in the Cloud, access is assured, no matter what occurs.

Proofs of the benefits rest in the opportunities this new technology represents. These opportunities should be taken advantage of. The benefits of online client accounting are available, and wise business owners and their accounting professionals should use them to their full potential.

So consider the benefits of Cloud computing for the accounting professional. Here are the facts:

Anytime, anywhere access:

- Access to your data 24/7 via an Internet connection

- Your offices can be located remotely

- Up-time is 99.98% of the time

Organizing information:

- For financial data: multi-user access to a full desktop version of accounting programs

- The ability to locate information and documents within seconds

- Improved time allocation: promoting efficiency and profitability in billable time

<u>Risk Management</u>

Security will always be a concern that must be addressed. Access to information truly is power. Security can never be taken for granted and it is closely related to risk management. In fact, security is built into online accounting. This is one of the additional benefits of working in the Cloud. Consider these operations:

RAID (Redundant Array of Independent Disks), premium

firewalls and routers, as well as 256-bit encryption at login, a secure portal and networks, enterprise level firewalls, and a state of the art data center operating 24/7, provide users with on-site monitoring and security.

A Network Operations Center (NOC) team monitors for potential threats and sabotage at all times. A fully staffed NOC monitors for earthquakes, severe weather, and IP Address intrusions, to name some. The data center has an uninterrupted power supply to ensure that users experience no downtime.

To ensure premium enterprise services, reliability, and security for all data center infrastructure, systems should have N+1 / 2N (or greater) redundancy levels. "2N redundancy" is a term used to describe two identical systems where everything is duplicated and monitored at multiple locations. This kind of highly designed system integration eliminates any single points of failure and immediately institutes total redundancy and a fail-over plan. In short, if one system fails to work for any reason, the other one kicks in. Please see Chapter 10, *Virtual Can Be Reality,* Data Centers.

Managing security risks takes several forms. For one, only authorized users have access to information. Another: the administrator can turn this access on and off according to need.

Management of risk is no longer optional. Control of "who sees what and when they see it" is a paramount consideration.

Online accounting mitigates if not eliminates the risks of compromised financial data.

We will cover more about Security in Chapter 7, *Cloud Computing—Easy, Convenient, Secure.*

Solving the Headaches of Accountants and Businesses

Accounting professionals face business headaches that working together in the Cloud can solve. The goal, of course, is to get the job done, and get it done right, without undue interference from built-in or external inhibitors.

One issue is accessing the accounting software easily which includes accounting files, databases, and spreadsheets. With the Cloud, the need to create and send these kinds of files back and forth is eliminated.

Next, sharing information: the Cloud provides a central location for documents that can be accessed anytime and anywhere.

Accountants may often need remote access to their client's computer. The information was not in a centralized location. The client and the accountant could not access the same computer at the same time. Speed was extremely slow and security could be compromised. But with the Cloud, these inhibitors are eliminated. The client's computer doesn't have to be on, multiple users can access the same file at the same time, speed and convenience are increased, and security is built in.

How about data backup? Normally companies do not back up their data on a daily basis, even though they should, and whether they do or not, the data is either stored offsite or on CD's. Checking the integrity of back up files can be difficult and time consuming. Weigh the ease and convenience of backing up data in the Cloud: it's there, it's current, and it's always accessible.

Too many accounting professionals spend non-billable time installing software updates. It's a needless cost-center for the accountant, not to mention a waste of time.

With the Cloud, software updates are performed by the Managed Service Provider/Hosting Service Provider, and in a dedicated virtual server environment the access can be given to the client as well.

Already referenced but again highlighted here: the Cloud may eliminate the need to have an IT consultant on staff. The cost savings could be immense.

Before the Cloud, business owners would contact accounting professionals "after the fact," practicing a reactive response. Usually business professionals need answers quicker, preferably in real time. With the Cloud, real time access to answers is reality.

Everyone knows technology is constantly changing. Keeping informed about the changes that affect accounting operational efficiencies has been time consuming, and non-billable. Not anymore: with the Cloud, information is more readily accessible, can be acquired and applied quickly, and the accountant can continue to do what he or she is paid to do.

Finally for this list: anyone can work from virtually anywhere. All that is needed is an Internet connection. Freeing an accountant from a desk ideally allows that individual to complete his or her work sooner so that family time doesn't remain just a dream.

5

Facts and Impacts—Resistance to Change

Consider the methods you and your company teams employ now if they are *not* using the Cloud. Do these questions resonate with you?

- Are your servers located on-site, at the office?

- Do you retain an IT professional on staff?

- Do you have access to IT help when your office is closed?

- Do you continue to have to acquire software updates and new licenses for use?

- Is your business knowledgeable as to which software programs to purchase and install, which licenses to acquire, or do you have to hire a competent person to help you fulfill these needs?

- Are you ever not able to contact a competent IT professional when you need his or her services the most?

- Does your current IT system have redundancy in case of a failure and loss of information or access?

- Do you maintain your existing hardware until it simply dies, and has to be replaced?

- Do you have to hire a contractor to replace it?

- Is your disaster recovery shaky at best?

- How limited is your access to professionals upon whom your business depends, like your accountants? Are accounting tasks done remotely where speed and security can be sacrificed, or do these tasks have to be done by an accountant who physically has to come to your office?

What if you and your employees moved to the Cloud? Perhaps you are already convinced of the benefits. Would there be any pushback from your people?

Resistance to change is usually driven by insecurity, and that insecurity is usually driven by a lack of education, a willingness to learn, or a fear of failure. These are some of the reasons educating people about the Cloud is so important.

Resistance: The Top Five Reasons

Consider the top five reasons offered from prospects who resist moving to the Cloud:

1. They already have a server and want to wait for it to die— the exact opposite of a proactive stance that anticipates the future and embraces methods to prepare for and enhance success.

2. Fear of the unknown—"we've always done it the other way"—the attitude that keeps businesses from growing.

3. Security concerns—the features of encryption and authorized access will replace the doubts surrounding security, and no small-to-medium-sized business could re-create the enterprise security levels of a certified Cloud host.

4. Not understanding how new technology will work— continual education is the only answer for ignorance.

5. People who are not convinced of the benefits of Cloud computing who therefore cannot sell what they doubt will

work—when computing in the Cloud is proven beneficial, people have to be educated and convince themselves, and then commit to new actions based on verifiable information.

Now think of the differences and the benefits of computing in the Cloud. Let's take the first list above for comparison.

- Servers are not located at your site and redundancies are built in so that when disaster strikes, service remains un-interrupted.

- There is nothing wrong with retaining an IT professional on staff, of course, depending on the size of your business. However, many see the value of replacing this person with a team of individuals who work together in the Cloud, recognizing a considerable cost savings and an expansion of their billable services.

- Access to IT help and computing services is never un-reachable. In fact, it's available 24/7/365.

- Software updates are maintained by the help desk support of the Cloud vendor who also secures the necessary licenses.

- Hardware you have been using doesn't have to be replaced except perhaps the devices you use to access the Internet.

- Disaster recovery, because of redundancy, is assured.

- Access for professionals upon whom your business depends is a standard feature, and is accomplished securely

Embracing Change

Change is never accomplished in a vacuum. It is not filled with empty promises and dreams that cannot be defined or fulfilled. Change, if it is to be reliable, is accomplished best when facts are known, possibilities are limitless, and security is paramount.

People embrace it when it carries more than just hope. People embrace it when it is shown to be beneficial.

If resistance to change is a workplace condition, it must be addressed. The few should not hold back the many in terms of recognizing and achieving opportunities for success.

When the benefits of moving to the Cloud are compared to the hindrances of older work paradigms, positive change is not an option. It's a requirement.

This is the new work environment.

6

The New Work Environment

Cooperation between partners, vendors, clients, suppliers, and end users is the name of the game in a new and progressive work environment. The ability to share and collaborate with clients and partners is required in a fast paced and ever evolving work culture.

For cooperation to occur, an understanding must exist: this is working together, not working apart. This is joining hands, not putting up walls.

"Busy" Is the Paradigm

Most business owners are busy. Many time and money demands interrupt if not form the composition of their daily activities. These demands often act as inhibitors to cooperation.

So if "busy" is normal it should be matched by a commitment to cooperate by using time wisely, on the part of all the players.

Time is a valuable commodity. It has value depending on how it's used, of course. When used well it adds value to an enterprise. When it's used poorly it can eat up more than minutes and hours; it consumes money and energy, too. Time utilized more efficiently doesn't become or remain a cost center; in fact, its utilization can and should become a profit center.

A lot of time can be consumed just sending information back and forth to the people who need to access it, and that time represents money as well as energy expenditures. One thing about time: once it's used, it's gone and its value can only be seen in the residual effects of how it was spent.

How about an environment of cooperation where the time that was formerly used awkwardly to transfer information is now employed more efficiently (information transferred in real time), where cooperation and collaboration are enhanced?

Computing in the Cloud saves time for the business owner and his or her associates. It increases the chances for cooperation. Therefore, it saves energy and money for everyone involved.

In a new work environment saving and making the most of all three—time, energy, and money—is a huge plus to a business owner and his or her employees, partners, and customers. Enhancing cooperation is simply an added plus.

Mitigating the Risks

Any evolving work environment carries risks in its ongoing operations. One risk that business owners face regularly is in accessing and changing documents, especially if these documents contain sensitive information. What if a document can't be opened due to software or hardware problems? What if changes in another version of the same document don't match the changes in the original document stored on someone else's data base?

Computing in the Cloud allows access to documents including accounting files, spreadsheets, and word documents for all who need to see them. It allows the changes that need to be made to be incorporated without the hassles of searching multiple document locations and wondering if programs are interchangeable.

Another risk becomes a major nuisance in a work environment apart from the Cloud. Simply put, it is lack of communication (and that often affects cooperation). Too often it's simply hard to get a hold of the people who are needed to work on a project. Or, when they are accessed, it is difficult if not impossible to put everyone on the same page in order to accomplish agreed upon goals.

In the Cloud, people are able to reach each other conveniently and in real time, as well as access the information they need, and those two aspects alone carry great importance in saving time, energy and money.

In a work environment involving creating and accessing data on computer systems over the Internet, the requirements of security of access and maintaining privacy of information continue to remain paramount. Apart from the Cloud, risks rise disproportionately.

For example, if the wrong email address is used, or an email account is hacked, sensitive information can be retrieved on the Internet and shared with people who should not be part of the communication loop. Leaks of vital and sensitive data can destroy people and their production, not to mention a company or enterprise by giving away secrets to the highest bidder. People without access codes can breach even high walls of security—it happens all the time.

In the Cloud, however, secure portals are created in which documents can be deposited into a virtual "vault" in a virtual office environment where these documents "live." Access to them is granted only to those who must have it. Information is encrypted.

A business owner, his or her company accountants, and authorized employees can share most of the information at the same time when they log in—they don't have to "check documents in and out." Work is accomplished simultaneously and therefore more efficiently. These are parts of the ease and convenience of working together in the Cloud.

Business professionals usually run multiple programs on their desktops. The ability to share information with others in their company who need to know, can sometimes be relegated to whether or not another authorized party has access to the right desktop—and that can be a problem when two or more people try to access the desktop at the same time.

The Cloud solves this problem, providing secure access to programs and documents simultaneously. When authorized people work together in these ways, ideas and solutions are generated. They can be weighed and evaluated, and then upon agreement, applied to the problems at hand. All participants come away better for the experience, security remains strong, and former frustrations are reduced if not eliminated.

Updates from software suppliers can be unnerving when they interrupt daily work flow patterns. When these updates become available, production can stop or be slowed as the whole organization installs them, even though people are told "you can continue working."

In the Cloud, updates happen regardless, continually, and work production is not inhibited. Remember, the larger the organization is, the less time an owner or manager wants to dedicate to maintain business applications. Working in the Cloud is a tremendous asset in this regard—using less time to maintain applications means more time to create profits.

The Crashing Computer and No Redundancy

William is a business owner. His company employs 36 people in a rapidly growing industrial manufacturing industry and he has been moderately successful in an extremely challenging economic downturn. His Profit and Loss statements show some strength but really more resilience in fighting the uphill battle to stay afloat and make the profits he knows are needed to maintain and grow his business.

William tries to run a tight ship. He tries to be computer and IT-efficient. He has a file server, an application server, and an email server at his office.

One of his immediate challenges is securing additional funding for his company, to meet the needs of a contract worth $50,000.00. To accomplish this goal he needs to run financial statements for his bank. The bank has set a time requirement in place—they need financial statements for their funding committee to review by Friday at 3:00 PM.

On this Friday morning William endeavors to access the information to prepare the documentation he needs. His applications open but when he tries to open his file server, it doesn't respond. He notices that his file server is off and will not boot up. Frustrated, he remembers that his technology expert is currently on vacation and won't return to the office until the following Monday.

He decides to locate another person who can discover what is wrong with the file server and repair it. He calls a couple of people and learns that the soonest anyone can make an office call is Saturday—one day too late.

Further investigation reveals that a piece of hardware has failed. To remedy this problem, new equipment has to be ordered and the promised delivery date is Wednesday the following week!

His business is dependent on access to these files. His commitment to acquire and fulfill a $50,000.00 contract is also dependent on these files. This situation is not good.

The costs are potentially enormous to him and his firm. His business will be slowed, or perhaps shut down altogether for up to six days, his deadline with the bank will not be met, his immediate request for funding will not be reviewed, and in the process he likely will lose a lucrative contract.

If William had located his business data systems in the Cloud, a redundant file server would have made a transition seamless, his financial statements would have been prepared and delivered on time, he wouldn't have been beholden to the vacation time schedule of his IT person, nor the vendor for work on a Saturday, nor the delivery time frame of Wednesday the next week for the new equipment to replace the old. Plus, his business would have continued to function, the likelihood of securing the major contract would have increased, and his levels of personal and professional frustration would have been drastically reduced.

The story of a disaster recovery plan is like writing the future for an inevitable outcome. The question is not if disaster or negative circumstances will strike; the question is when these problems will come and whether or not a business is prepared with a secure plan that provides seamless transition when the ugly future rears its head.

The Cloud offers the redundancy that an organization needs in times of IT crisis. The vendor chosen by the customer is available and the disaster recovery plan is in place. The simple assurance of this fact provides internal comfort and security that some would say is a good investment no matter the upfront costs.

Cost Comparisons

The infrastructure costs of solving situations like these by yourself or in-house, could be between $50,000.00 and $100,000.00 when you consider all the factors in the story above. Costs of losses certainly depend on the number of users, but the point remains: why pay them if you don't have to?

For larger firms the losses could go much higher, to a midscale of a quarter million dollars. If potential losses like these are planned for and money is set aside, well, perhaps no worries. But in a struggling economy, few small businesses can plan for these contingencies and set aside the funds to mitigate the losses when disaster strikes.

For those organizations that don't possess resources in these amounts, including the time and the knowledge bases to meet negative circumstances head-on, the Cloud offers a virtual server solution where the business owner or division manager has the upper hand. The leader is the administrator of the solution, not the searcher for one in the midst of a crisis.

Because this leader works in the Cloud, he or she has set up multiple redundant operational systems and has backup off-site and within their control. These resources can literally constitute life or death factors for a business in environments where so much time, energy, and money are leveraged because there may be no alternative options.

Probably no one would argue that a new business environment brings new information creation, storage, retrieving, and sharing challenges. For those who work together in the Cloud, their costs of maintaining and growing success ratios are less, and the chances of earning more and keeping it are high. These factors alone cause savvy business owners and their employees to consider the benefits of the Cloud.

7

Cloud Computing—Easy, Convenient, Secure

Let's review: Cloud computing is becoming popular because it is easy, convenient, and security is high. The economics make sense, too. The idea and the reality of working from anywhere make availability and accessibility of virtual environments possible. Again, all that is needed is an Internet connection.

Potential users compare their old methods with new Cloud methods and see that the comparisons speak for themselves. For the majority of businesses, moving to the Cloud is the preferred option because the traditional methods have simply worn out or have worn their users out.

Processing information in the Cloud incorporates some of

the attributes of work production only dreamt before the 1980's. It is important to note some of these plus factors.

First, a lower cost of ownership and user-ship is a prime motivator. Computer hardware may not be inexpensive. Replacing it takes a toll on valuable resources. Ways of reducing costs of capital expenditures must always play a part in the consideration of business operations. Plus, the costs of hiring and retaining professional staff to manage computer hardware have to be considered. It can be concluded that in terms of costs of production and people, moving to the Cloud, in most instances, will save money for a business owner even though computer hardware has to be replaced every so often.

Second, many risks are lowered if not mitigated completely. Risks involving data storage and accessibility, security concerns over which documentation can be accessed and reviewed, and those of file sharing, are on the list of reduced or eliminated threats.

So it is reasonable for a business professional to ask, "What will Cloud computing do for my company?" Do you know what I mean? Basically, what business owner would not want to invest in and utilize a computing environment where less money was spent and security was tight?

Who Is Together in the Cloud?

The list of the types of individuals who are working together in the Cloud is expanding. Here are a few examples:

1. Business owners

2. Company employees

3. Sales staff

4. Accounting personnel

5. Business consultants

6. Investors

7. Private individuals

These and many more discover and utilize benefits that include but are definitely not limited to ease of access, convenience, security, cost savings, as well as accurate and time sensitive reporting. When one considers this simple list, it all makes sense.

What Is Driving Cloud Computing?

The conditions that drive cloud computing for business professionals contain the most common and essential business practice consideration and models of efficiency.

As you would well imagine, economics is the primary one as noted before. It simply costs less to use the Cloud than it does computing in a more traditional fashion. To be conservative, typically the cost savings is between 30% and 70%.

Next, speed comes into play, a part of the ease of computing. The Cloud is faster and simpler to use. As noted above, instant and secure access, real time collaboration, and not having to move files back and forth are all cost reducers, and potential profit enhancers. The bottom line: traditional methods of computing use desktops and local resources. In the Cloud, Cloud server resources are used. For many, this kind of simplicity is where savings of time and money start and continue.

Data back-up and server redundancies are solid considerations, too. These go hand in hand with in-place disaster recovery plans that are prepared to kick in when the inevitable negative circumstances come along.

The Cloud is eco-friendly in that it replaces the servers and their energy consumption on a client's site with combined energy usage at another, saving money and energy for the user. Plus, the Cloud is paperless, saving on ink and toners, too. Saving energy, personal and environmental, is always a plus.

Key Technology Drivers

Impetus to move to Cloud computing comes from many sources. Key technology drivers encourage users to consider a new work environment. Among them:

1. Security

2. Technical Support

3. Virtual Server Technology

4. Real Time Unified Communication

5. Remotely Managed IT

6. Managed Hosting and Types of Clouds

7. Private and Public Clouds

8. Virtual Servers vs. Shared Environments

9. Document Management

Security

Because not every risk can be completely eliminated in any environment, it is vital that security is on the top of the list for anyone who wants to compute in the Cloud. Cloud computing possesses several high security features. One is maintaining the highest security available.

Certification along many platforms is constantly updated as new security measures become part and parcel of an up-to-date data center. A recognized and independent auditing standard must be employed that includes a uniform format for reporting. It must demonstrate that an organization has participated in an in-depth audit of their objectives and activities which often includes controls over IT processes and financial reporting. When data is hosted or processed by a third party over the Internet, adequate controls and safeguards must be in place.

Another security feature currently is 256-bit encryption for data. Encryption is simply a means to not allow unauthorized people to see data they shouldn't see.

When a user accesses the Cloud, standard security log on requirements are in play. One is a first username and password for an online portal. Another is a second username and password for some applications. This is especially true in accounting where an accounting professional has to access a customer's financial files.

Additionally, a reliable Cloud server operation will maintain 24/7/365 security staff on-site, and redundancy of all data and data center systems.

While no human security effort is going to be completely fool proof, these measures make Cloud computing one of the most reliable and secure forms of doing business.

Technical Support

Everyone needs this at some point. Or at least a person needs to know that technical support is available at any time. Reliable vendors of Cloud computing hosting will provide technical support no matter the case or the cause as long as it's for the server or data center and not for local machines.

One aspect of technical support is being able to access a help desk whenever you need to, knowing that the help desk is continually staffed with knowledgeable people dedicated to helping you solve the technical issues that arise.

You have to be able to count on this. Make sure you deal with a vendor with a help desk that meets your requirements.

Virtual Server Technology

Virtual server technology is sometimes known as "on demand software." Basically it means that software is being delivered in a hosted Cloud environment that is accessed by users over the Internet. Virtual server technology is important to clients for several reasons.

1. There is no need to install, maintain, or update software.

2. The latest version can be running at all times.

3. The client doesn't need to update or spend time changing software.

4. Pricing is generally all-inclusive. The client pays one price for multiple benefits.

5. Information can be accessed through secure portals with 256-bit encryption.

6. Data is backed up through a redundancy of servers in a constantly updated data center. Here, as noted, an audit has been performed by a third-party organization, assuring that infrastructure, financial statements, the data facilities, and data processing services have undergone objective scrutiny. The benefits are legitimacy and reduced opportunities for "cooking the books" where financial data is concerned.

7. There is no maintenance of software and servers at a local site, and this usually means a lowering of the IT budget.

Real Time Unified Communication

Real Time simply means "as it actually happens." People

communicating in real time are far more likely to be able to process collaborative information quicker and with greater efficiency. Interested parties (business owners, financial professionals, consultants, clients) simply communicate better when they are together in the Cloud.

No matter the applications being used, this kind of across-the-board instantaneous communication can be accomplished with a single login interface. Access and availability in real time provide everyone with the information they need when they need it.

The applications that can be used in the Cloud in real time are many. Consider these and many are industry-specific:

1. Accounting software

2. Tax software

3. Spreadsheets

4. Financial planning software

5. Applications that are "stand alone" and those that are "add on"

6. Document management (including word and data documents)

7. Email exchange

8. Proprietary software

9. PDF's

10. Customer relationship management

Options exist in the Cloud that may be limited only by the software that is currently available. Because software is constantly being invented or upgraded, the Cloud is a user-friendly environment so these applications can be accessed and utilized in their most current versions.

Remotely Managed IT

The on-site IT manager may not reside at your local site any more. Instead of a person at a physical location managing an in-house server, management is being done at a different, off-site location. That location, of course, is the Cloud, and that location probably resides at different data centers throughout the US.

The bottom line here: no physical presence is required to maintain IT infrastructure.

Managed Hosting and Types of Clouds

Managed hosting is simply "managing the hardware and

software infrastructure." Often this term is used in conjunction with discussions about the types of Clouds that are available.

When traveling and speaking, I often hear this: "I am not in the Cloud." Or I hear, "What is Cloud Computing?" I always love to ask this question: "Do you use Cloud Computing?" I hear many answers, but most often, "No." Or, "What's that?"

I think it is important to understand the different types of clouds. The more familiar we are with these, the more we will find ourselves together with our heads in the Cloud!

What's in the Cloud? Diagram

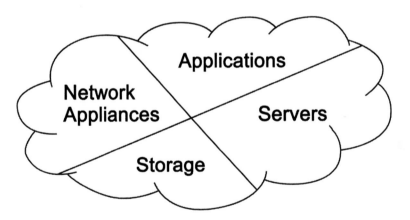

There are basically three types of cloud computing:

- Software as a Service—this is the most widely used and is also known as SaaS. Software as a Service is used in a web browser. It is not locally installed on your desktop or in the Cloud.

SaaS eliminates worries about application servers, storage servers, application development, and other related concerns of IT. This is the most common software for Internet email, online banking, and instant messaging.

SaaS is commonly used where a vendor is delivering an online edition of their product. It is important to note that if there is a desktop version of the application, the SaaS edition is usually different and has limited functionality.

- Infrastructure as a Service—known of as IaaS, this provides the platform to virtualized servers on which users can install applications; i.e. accounting software, tax programs, customer relationship programs, document readers, spreadsheets, and word processing software.

  The benefit of this is that you can access information anytime and anywhere if done correctly. However, the need to maintain the infrastructure is your responsibility in most cases. An important fact: most of the time it is an art to take desktop applications to the cloud and a reliable vendor is necessary.

- Platform as a Service—abbreviated PaaS, is also known as Provision Hosting or as Application Software Provider

(ASP). This provides the virtualization of servers, networks, and storage in the Cloud.

The benefits include accessing accounting software, tax programs, customer relationship programs, document readers, spreadsheets, and word processing software. Again, this comes with the benefits of accessing information anytime and anywhere.

However, the biggest benefit is the management of the hardware, the use of secure data centers, and the installation of software. When considering Platform as a Service, it is important to do business with an authorized commercial provider.

Private and Public Clouds

There are basically two types of clouds that I consider to be viable. One is "private" and the other is "public."

A "private" Cloud essentially is cloud computing capability dedicated to a single organization. The cloud computing software is dedicated only to the customer's company, hence the term "private."

A "public" Cloud is Cloud computing capability and resources that are shared by multiple organizations. The equipment, infrastructure, and cloud computing software are not dedicated only to the customer's company.

This leads us to a brief discussion on Virtual Servers vs. Shared Environments.

Virtual Servers vs. Shared Environments

Options exist for the business who wants to work together in the Cloud. One is to consider the differences and benefits of virtual servers versus shared environments.

A shared environment is one that shares servers and applications among users. Files are not shared, of course, but resources are. The Cloud takes the server and cookie cuts it into a folder infrastructure consisting of "trees" or "modules." These folders are then secured for each individual according to the policies established by the user. Each folder and often individual files utilize their own security access features so that users can be confident that no one else who is sharing the resources of the virtual server environment has access to their files.

A dedicated environment is what is commonly referred to as Private Cloud Solutions. This is where a business has purchased their own virtual server to host their data, applications, and users in one central location. Only that company's users can access the server to utilize the given resources.

It is important to note here that a virtual server is not to say it's a dedicated piece of hardware, although that is available as well. "Virtual server" means that a portion of the hardware has been partitioned off to create a private server for the business. This server has its own allotment of resources specifically for those users, and their own IP address to login to.

Kacee Johnson writes, "Private servers are great because they give the owner much more freedom and flexibility. They also allow for faster tech solutions because the client can determine when the server has backups running and when the server has reboots performed. If an issue develops that needs to be resolved, the tech team will know exactly where to look."

I recommend the use of a dedicated environment. Some opinions exist that encourage consideration and utilization of a "hybrid" of shared and dedicated environments but I see no need for these. By far the most secure, easiest, and convenient one for any use is a dedicated, exclusive-only-to-them environment. Here there is greater and enhanced flexibility, and any changes will not affect other organizations. The converse is also true: since no one else has access to a dedicated environment except the user to whom it is dedicated, changes in other environments made by other organizations will in no way affect the owner of the dedicated environment.

Document Management

In the Cloud, we have a paperless environment, which in addition to energy savings, is eco-friendly. Information doesn't need to be printed out. It's accessed and reviewed in the Cloud and reports can be updated without printers, ink costs, and equipment use and maintenance.

Think of the savings. Key technology drivers motivate businesses to move to the Cloud. For some, the question may not be "Should we?" but, "When, and how?"

8

Initiate, Innovate, and Implement

By now, it may be easier to see why many transition to the Cloud for their computing. Initiating needful change like this promotes innovation, and implementation of new ideas is what positive change is all about.

Positive change carries inherent possibilities along with risks—this is obvious. But the more a person is educated and understands both possibilities and risks, the greater is the chance of making informed choices that really make sense.

History of the Progression of Change

Perhaps a brief history lesson will help us understand the progression of change. In the 1980's we were introduced to Internet Service Provider (ISP) 1.0. The ISP provided access to the Internet via dial-up, ISDN (Integrated Services Digital Network), and T1 and T3 fiber optics.

Then in the early 1990's we were introduced to ISP 2.0 where access to servers was located at the Internet access point. Co-location, ISP 3.0, came into play around the same time where racks for your equipment were located at the Internet access point.

ASP (Application Software Provider, ISP 4.0) gave birth to SaaS (Software as a Service) Internet-based applications and services in the mid-1990's (what we have called Virtual Server Technology). The Cloud concept (ISP 5.0) came about in the mid-2000s.

Currently 5% of small businesses use Cloud services in the United States. Within three years I predict that usage in the United States could be as high as 40%. Others will follow as computing in the Cloud catches on. The growth will be dramatic over the next several years, as this bell curve shows.

Dramatic Growth Bell Curve Diagram

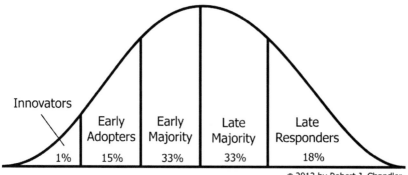

© 2012 by Robert J. Chandler

The Cloud provides dynamic, Internet-optimized infrastructure for hosting applications. There is no limit to the possibilities, and they are still unfolding.

It's easy to see the progression. While the seeds of change have been around for a long time, the technology has improved from year to year as you would expect it would and more and more people are taking advantage of it.

Improvements have helped business owners and managers speed up performance through utilizing multiple applications in the Cloud. Efficiencies from a cost standpoint have increased. Savvy businesses can now move their whole operations to the Cloud instead of dealing with just single applications at one time.

Is It Time to Initiate Change and Implement?

Ultimately the leader of the organization makes the decision to move to the Cloud, or not. The factors he or she employs, as well as the information that is accessed and evaluated will help the progressive leader choose the best options.

If an organization wants to transition to the Cloud, certain considerations must be weighed. One, is the assessment of the risks—perceived and real.

Cloud Computing Fears and How to Address Them

When risks are weighed, one question that pops up is basically this: "What could go wrong?" So, let's take a look at this question. Several factors play into it. Perception can be reality for many and risk is closely associated with fear.

- **Cost:** "It costs too much." Really? Many cloud computing companies offer monthly, quarterly, and annual agreements. Ask yourself: "What would it cost to build a data center or data centers, and how much capacity would be required for redundancy of application, storage and email servers, and back-ups off-site?" The great benefit is that you purchase cloud "seats" and resources as you need them.

- **Knowledge:** "It's too hard, and I don't understand how it works." Well, think back to the cell phone and recall when you picked up the cell phone for the first time. You made a call, then you probably entered a contact into your phone, then you searched the Internet, and then you checked your email, and then you texted your friend. As your comfort level rose, the cell phone became a device you could not live without and your learning curve was quick.

- **Interoperability:** "What happens when everything

doesn't work together? What if my Application Provider is still trying to understand how *their* software works in the Cloud?" Delivering applications in the Cloud *can* sometimes be challenging; therefore, the developer of the software should have experience with the Cloud and how their software will perform within it.

- **Control:** "I like to have control and I cannot see my data or server in the Cloud like I can at my office. Control gives me peace of mind." Are you currently doing back-ups daily? What happens if a natural disaster takes place? Is your information in a different location, and what is your current disaster recovery plan? In the Cloud, you have access to your data anytime, anywhere; therefore, if need be you can copy documents from the Cloud to your local computer. Also, many Cloud computing providers will provide a backup for a nominal fee.

- **Support:** "Getting tech support is too difficult. I prefer to have an IT person I can talk to." How long does it currently take you to get an IT person on-site? What happens if your IT professional goes on vacation, gets sick, or decides to leave the company, what is next? Most cloud providers offer 24/7/365 help desk support, live chat, and a knowledge base to provide instant answers to your issues within minutes, not hours or days.

- **Internet Failure:** "What if the Internet goes down?" If your Internet goes down at your office, you would be down due to most networking setups even without being in the Cloud. When you are in the Cloud and your Internet goes down, you just go to a local coffee vendor location with Internet access, or your local library, and you are back up!

- **Cloud Company Out of Business:** "If my Cloud hosting company goes out of business, what are my options?" This question is why researching your vendors, is important. If a Cloud vendor is accredited by MSP Alliance then they have gone through the gambit of background evaluations both technically and fiscally, giving clients the security and assurance that it is a veteran company and will be around.

- **Computer Hacking:** "What if my system gets hacked into?" Hackers, unfortunately, will always try to hack systems—even including the Pentagon! However, if you are with an Enterprise level Cloud provider, they will have security systems in place to recognize the hacking attempts and shut down IP addresses or even full countries. If you were to have a hacker attempt to access your information stored on a local system, you would not have the system monitoring in place to identify these attempts so a successful hacking attempt is much more likely on a local system than on an enterprise solution.

- **Implementation and Training Are Difficult:** "I need help because I am not good with technology." Knowledge is power. Take the time to follow the implementation steps below and you will find that the Cloud is very user friendly.

Understanding, weighing, and dealing with concerns like these requires knowledge. The more a user or client knows, the more secure they are in mitigating perceived or real fear factors.

Phases of Implementation

Implementation takes time and it should be done in phases. Making the time to implement these important changes, assuring that they are done correctly is right.

Businesses moving to the Cloud need to prepare as they consider what is really in store. Understanding and proceeding through the phases of implementation sequentially help to insure the quality of a smooth transition to the Cloud.

Here are the phases and their time lines. Know these and adapt them to your business:

Phase 1

(Time line is 7-10 days):

- *Get your questions answered.* Deal with a Cloud service vendor that is willing to talk with you. Make sure they are licensed commercial hosts, vetted with experience.

- *Understand which environment is best for your business.* List your needs, interview hosts on capabilities, and then decide on which vendor is the best fit for your company, determined by their service offerings.

- *Test, test, test—to ensure a good fit for your firm.* Test speed, delivery, downloads, and printing and security, giving you a sound mind with your decision prior to paying out for licensing.

- *Speak to references.* Understand how long they have been on the system, how they are using it, and any recommendations they have on implementing.

- *Understand pricing.* Many vendors have hidden fees for storage or licensing, so be sure you understand fully all of the facets of the expenses prior to purchasing.

Phase 2

(Time line is 3-5 days):

- *Submit information on licensing and obtain user permissions.* This information consists of applications to be hosted as well as individual user permissions for applications and files.

- *Schedule date of launch.* Depending on the type of environment that you choose, this could be one day later or two weeks later. Take into consideration the migration of data and create a starting point for staff and clients.

- *Test local ISP connections and service.* Measure the bandwidth of your local Internet connection as well as the quality, packets lost, and the amount of "hops" you must take to get to the data center.

- *Update local print drivers and ensure that all updates are current.* It's very important to have the latest drivers as well as current service packs installed on your machine to ensure the best Cloud experience. Cloud technologies are created on the latest and greatest software available so old programs may not be optimal.

- *Soft launch with internal staff.* Before putting your clients on a system that is new to you, I recommend getting all of your staff on the system, first. Become comfortable with it and work out any bugs internally then train your clients.

- *Test software, security, and printing to ensure that there are no bugs.* In moving to any new server you may have to make tweaks. This process just allows you the time to ensure all questions are answered and that staff are working efficiently.

- *Set up scanners.* Ensure they are TWAIN-compliant prior to purchase—TWAIN is the interface standard that allows imaging hardware devices to communicate with image processing software. Scanning to the Cloud is easy, but it's important that you purchase scanners that are compatible versus cheaper options that may not be.

- *Add an embedded link to your website for login.* If you plan on having clients login, it's a nice feature to allow for direct sign-on from your own website as you are able to drive more traffic to your site, brand your company, and create a community for users.

- *Acquire ongoing and in-depth training.* I always recommend that you stay abreast with new information, especially when dealing with technology as updates and upgrades will continually become available.

Phase 3

(Time line is one week):

- *Send information to your clients to get them set up.* A "Getting Started Guide" with usernames, passwords, and links to resources provides a good start. Private label the guides with your information. This gives your clients that extra touch that goes a long way.

- *Communicate regularly on resources and utilization.* Subscribe and register for updates and information from your provider, to stay current on information. It's a good idea to connect via social media outlets as well.

Phase 4

(Time line is ongoing):

- *Create a marketing plan to expand your horizons.* The Cloud removes all geographic boundaries on clientele you can service and when, so create a marketing plan to use the Cloud in a way that grows your business and offers new services.

- *Implement your sales team and the plan.* Ensure everyone is on the same page and educating clients with a consistent message.

The leader takes the initiative once he or she is convinced of the positive merits of the enterprise. The leader's team engages in innovation as it implements a transition to the Cloud. All of this begins with leadership that is demonstrated through decision making and proper implementation.

<u>Personal and Professional Benefits</u>

Implementation in the Cloud should have professional and personal benefits. Leaders who move their organizations to the Cloud should experience both.

Consider this story:

In 2010 a busy accountant from New York City came to a Cloud service provider with the hopes of moving her business to the Cloud and creating the luxury of retiring to paradise within two years. The hustle and bustle of the Big Apple was home, but not the place that she envisioned enjoying her golden years. She truly wanted to be able to work on her laptop from the beach wherever her sails had taken her.

She purchased a dedicated virtual server to host her clients accounting files and then later added a 3rd party application to it to track her time and billing. She quickly realized that the system was even more seamless than she had imagined and decided it was a great medium to acquire new clients on the portal from anywhere.

Her geographic boundaries were lifted so she began looking to get a few more clients from other areas of the world. Her goal was not to grow a large firm; rather, to have enough clients to create a sufficient income, allowing her to afford the luxury of her new lifestyle, travelling the world. She was a true believer in the "work smarter, not harder" methodology!

Growing her users from ten to eighteen in less than a year, she quickly realized that she had acquired enough business to begin her journeys to paradise sooner rather than later. Eighteen months after the launch of her server she formed her plans to begin the move to the South Pacific. From there she will be able to run her practice from her laptop on the beach.

This is a success story about how the Cloud allowed a client, a leader with vision, to expand her service offerings, her numbers of clientele, and her ease of access. An added plus: the Cloud also helped her succeed in her personal goals.

9

Leadership on the Line

It was during the 1950's when the word *online* was first used. Originally the word was used an adjective, or an adverb. Then it became a noun.

Online morphed into the "place" we know now as the world-wide web. Everyone even remotely acquainted with Internet technology or email possesses some degree of acquaintance with the term and uses it often in multiple applications.

Words and their meanings change over time, of course. Perhaps you recall the days when the word *keyboard* referred to the part of the acoustic piano the player touched with his or her fingers to make a sound that came from wooden hammers striking strings, and the term *dashboard* referred to the front portion of your car that contained your speedometer, odometer, and gas gauge. Remember when the word *blackberry* was a fruit? Terms' meanings and applications change as society invests and appropriates new meanings into them.

Online has changed and so has the leader's role regarding it. In fact, in a real sense, your leadership regarding online applications (adjective) and working online (noun) or being online savvy (adverb) is directly connected to how *you* line up with, or position yourself in opposition to, fundamental leadership principles that are as old as humanity itself. A leader's actions will, or will not, line up with ongoing responsibilities as society continues to change the meanings and applications of words.

If you are the leader, consider your role as you move your company toward an environment of more productivity, increased profit, reduced overhead, and acquiring accelerated profits. For those who grew up viewing television cartoons that featured characters that flew in to "save the day" (and there are many who still do) some might wonder that *every* problem faced by any superhuman or highly animated animal could be solved on TV within thirty minutes or less. It was amazing. But that fact certainly doesn't translate into real life working environments and the myriad of issues contemporary leaders and their companies face every day.

"Working smarter, not harder" is no longer a simple catch

phrase. It is the goal of every successful leader. This is especially true as you consider the benefits of being together in the Cloud with others of your company and your hosting organization.

We know resistance to change may be natural. To those who know that change is not optional, resistance doesn't become the standard of staying stuck, or the excuse for doing nothing. Enter the cartoon character with the huge red cape? No, enter the leader who knows how to lead well.

Leaders Set the Pace

"Leaders set the pace because they create it..." according to author Glen Aubrey in *Leadership Is—How to Build Your Legacy*, page 23. Leaders are not passive when it comes to embracing new and accurate information and acting upon it. From his book, *L.E.A.D.—Learning, Education, Action, Destiny*, page 27: "Leadership is present when the one in charge takes initiative. Without initiative, a leadership vacuum exists. No excuses— innovation, creativity, and activity replace complacency, whining, and mediocrity. The person who doesn't live in the latter will lead in the former.

"Understanding what to do, how to do it and the realistic expectations of results when proper initiative is applied are parts of a leader's quest for winning. Changes of behavior are required. They start with the leader.

119

"Leaders who want improvements do something, set the pace, and forge the paths. They act. They substitute wallowing in less than desirable circumstances with positive actions born of winning attitudes."

The leader's responsibilities are many, and growing. Among them are these, related to four characteristics of growing a healthy business:

- Values: identify the core truths that hold a company together, define them for the company, and demonstrate them in daily actions.

- Vision: see it, cast it, and cause it to come about.

- Mission: accomplish the goals of business.

- Message: live out and tell the truths that cause us to succeed.

Many years ago I became acquainted with these four principles. Through understanding these truths and using them, I learned how leaders truly lead well and that leadership is not an inherent trait, or a personality-borne characteristic. Leadership is, first of all, a decision about someone else's success and it is founded upon and driven by a fundamental truth. It is this: People are more important than production.

The leader who embraces that truth sees his or her people

with different eyes and becomes fundamentally aware that all people are basically wired the same way. Since that's true, the opportunities to lead well are not matters of guesswork; they are matters of working with what you know already works.

There is no challenge between people that cannot be addressed by values, vision, mission, and message. The key is to make sure that in any business enterprise, the four marks of what Aubrey calls The Code of Achievement, are known and activated. They work because of the opportunity that every day presents: to treat your people as you wish to be treated, and as you wish them to treat your customers. It's the Golden Rule that ultimately provides more than a level playing field—it's the gateway to gold, too.

Relationship and Function

Another rock solid principle that I learned is that relationships come before and give birth to function. Defining these two terms is important. According to *Leadership Is—How to Build Your Legacy*:

- A *relationship* is the decision I make about your success.

- A *function* is the action that proves the validity of the relationship.

If I am the leader I must set the pace (or I *will* set the pace of any activity whether I want to, or not). Therefore, it is my demonstration of the truth of the principles that forges the paths upon which others in my company will walk.

It is true that what they see me *do* has far more impact and long lasting residual effects than anything I *say*. Words, to be effective, have to be followed by deeds, or else they are expressions that are filling up dead air.

Leaders Change Their Behaviors, First

As the leader, I have to change my behavior before I desire, expect, or require someone else to change their behavior. If I make a decision about a staff member's success it is not optional that I change my behavior. If the decision about that staff member's success means anything to me, I will demonstrate my decision in the treatment I choose to display in front of and on behalf of that person.

Take these principles and apply them to changing a business paradigm from working "as we always have" and moving to computing together in the Cloud. As the leader I have to ask myself these four questions, among many:

- What is my responsibility to cast the vision for any positive change?

- When should I do it?

- How should I model pro-activity instead of reactivity?

- What is my role in teaching my staff about the need for adaptability and positive change in relationships and functions?

When a company that is led by a visionary and relationally-driven leader makes the decision to move to working together in the Cloud, the leader has to answer those questions, perhaps like this:

- As the leader, my responsibility is to see the vision and cast it. Often this is done by asking questions that cannot be answered by a "yes" or "no." For example, "If it could be shown that working together in the Cloud would raise our profits and improve our functionality, what should we do?" Or, "Part of growing this company is freeing up our people to accomplish more and with less stress. How would you feel about a way of working that would accomplish both?" Vision casting causes the one with the vision to ask the questions to instill that vision into others so that they own it, too.

- Casting vision is an ongoing process. Therefore, do it all the time.

- My model of pro-activity will show others what I have learned and am learning. "I tried this and it worked. Let me show you what I learned. Tell me what you think when I am done with the demonstration." The leader who leads well is more interested in discovery than declaration. In other words, the leader shows the possibility and allows the follower to discover the benefits. While declaration sometimes has to be done, the far-preferred method is discovery. When team members discover the vision *as the leader casts it*, they begin to own the process because *they are included in the journey*.

- The leader's role is to *always* be open to new ideas based on solid ideals that promote positive changes and beneficial results—regardless of the source of those ideas. When the leader states that he or she is open, the leader demonstrates it especially when a staff member comes up with a new and better method of accomplishing a task. Therefore, the leader *teaches* that staff that openness to new methods is part of the fabric of the cloth of the company. It's woven into the very tissues of the organization's make up. Further, when a new idea is adopted it is the leader's role to take the initiative to be the best student of the new technology or method, and then train others to accomplish it *better than the leader ever could*.

> When team members discover the vision *as the leader casts it,*
> they begin to own the process because *they are included in the*
> *journey.design and implementation?*

Positive Change Doesn't Happen by Accident

Here's the bottom line: positive change doesn't just happen by accident. There is always cause and effect. There is always a case for consideration and growth.

Change constantly occurs all around us, of course, but that phenomenon does not mean that *my* company will embrace change automatically. To make positive change work, the leader who cares about the people as well as the production (in that order) will become the student who learns and therefore leads, will take the initiative to embrace positive change and cast the vision to others so that they, too, will embrace and employ it, will treat his or her staff as more important than what they do regardless of any resistance the staff may have to change at the outset, and will provide room in strategic thinking and planning for innovation. This integration of principled thought and decisive positive action become part of who the company is and what the company does.

Working together in the Cloud has merits on many levels for those who wish to see them. The internal reality of ease and convenience is obvious. What may be a little harder to understand is no matter what progress technology can help us achieve, people are still people, and will always be. Our wiring is inherent.

Technology becomes the preferred tool to help people accomplish more and do it with greater ease. Working *together* in the Cloud is far more than just function—it's the field of cultivating relationships, too. This is a formidable combination and a fruitful one. I can't think of any reason why a forward-thinking and forward-acting company would not embrace its benefits, can you?

10

Virtual Can Be Reality

"Virtualize" Everything?

Someone could rightly say, "Virtual is not reality." Well, in the ways most people understand the word *virtual*, that would normally be true.

In the Cloud, however, "Virtual *is* reality." The use of a virtual environment makes the user more productive in his or her real environment: the office or on-site workplace.

There really is little mystery about this. The Cloud is composed of off-site servers and applications that can be accessed by authorized users. In this sense, they are not "virtual" in that they exist in a real place in real time.

But the reality of utilizing a virtual working environment where capabilities for computing, data creation, storage, retrieval, document alteration, and distribution (sharing) with other authorized personnel is not only possible but preferred, makes thinking and acting in a virtual environment much more contributory to the reality of the product provision in the real environment.

In short, working together in the Cloud "virtualizes everything" to make the processes of work easier and more convenient.

A Virtual Office in the Cloud

"Work from anywhere you like—all you need is an Internet connection." You may hear, or express this phrase more and more as time goes on. Company office policies designed to integrate people and production may never fully allow "off-site" office acquisition and application for every worker, but the trend today clearly is moving in the direction of "less time in commute" and "more time in compute."

In other words, if access to an IT work environment is as easily achieved from an Internet connection close to you and these connections are becoming more available worldwide, then why travel to an office if your work can be done from any Internet location, like your home?

All-in-One Virtual Office Solutions

Many solutions have already been addressed in this book. Suffice to say here that if accessing these solutions helps a person have more control of how they allocate and spend their personal and professional time, why wouldn't a potential user take advantage of those options?

If the desire in fast paced and often consuming business environments is for a business professional to enjoy more time with his or her family, become more productive, save time, energy, and money, then it really makes little if any sense to not take advantage of these positive attributes of change.

The concept of "All-in-One Virtual Office Solutions" means that you can have access to your information anytime, anywhere. Along with co-workers, consultants and clients can access the information at the same time instead of sending information back-and-forth. This fact really represents ease and convenience.

How is this done? Applications and data are accessed in the *one* centralized location instead of your information being stored in different places which prevents users sharing information at the same time.

This is a powerful solution because all information is accessed in certified data centers, IT costs are reduced, plus the cost of hardware solutions is lowered.

But virtual office solutions *are* different—in scope, application, and profitability. They are different in that they *are* all-in-one. Because they are "virtual" and in combination provide additional possibilities for expansion and savings along the way, some people may fear the loss of control. Some may wager that if they "let go" somehow this new way of doing business will impede their progress, violate their security, and put their business' future at risk.

Well, consider the alternatives. The scope of virtual office solutions is limitless, no walls, no inhibitors, no brake pedals. The vitality of these all-in-one solutions, in the right environment, should free up the business owner or those with whom he or she works, to become more dedicated to the fulfilling the dreams of the business as opposed to wallowing in the reasons it may have struggled.

Applying "virtual" to your ways of working simply means accessing new technology and using it for your benefit as well as the benefit of those who work with you. The plusses and rewards are many as has been noted.

Where profitability becomes the child of more efficient business practices shown to be secure and already working, gaining the rewards simply may be the good and best choice for the business or individual who wants to move with technology and receive its merits.

It bears repeating: all you need is an Internet connection and login credentials, and you are on your way to working in the Cloud.

Virtual or Remote Desktop

A virtual or remote desktop is simply a desktop that is accessed in the Cloud. See what's *on* your desktop, only see it and access it not physically *at* your desktop; rather, from a more secure and virtual office environment anytime, anywhere.

Imagine it this way: in the Cloud (on the Internet) you see the desktop you may have always seen—it's just not being accessed on or from your local server. The programs are there, the files are there, but the access is "remote"—and therefore secure and managed by a vendor who is guaranteeing redundancy and reliability.

As I have stated, Cloud vendors provide a multiple range of services in this environment. One is software as a service, another infrastructure as a service, and the third is platform as a service. Together the options for online computing in the Cloud provide profound benefits in document storage and retrieval, document management, accounts payable and accounts receivable operations, customer relations management, project management, tax reporting, and document sharing in real time.

Virtual Servers

Virtual servers are created when a physical computer's software divides the computer into multiple isolated virtual environments. As noted before, these can be private, hybrid, or public. Also as noted before, I recommend dedicated environments and private Clouds.

The reality of utilizing a virtual working environment where capabilities for computing, data creation, storage, retrieval, document alteration, and distribution (sharing) with other authorized personnel is not only possible, but preferred. This fact makes thinking and acting in a virtual environment much more contributory to the reality of the product provision in the real environment.

In the final analysis, working together in the Cloud "virtualizes everything." It makes the processes of work easier and more convenient.

For clients looking for a more robust and reliable system, working together in the Cloud meets and exceeds those desires. Virtual servers have tremendous benefits.

Here are a few:

- They are cost effective for 10+ users.

- Any third party applications that are compatible can be installed on a customer's virtual server.

- There are no server maintenance costs.

- Freedom and flexibility are hallmarks of using virtual servers.

- Purchase options exist that allow customers to pay for and utilize only the resources they need, customizing their acquisitions, again saving time, energy, and money.

- Virtual servers are easily scalable, to increase and decrease resources during busy seasons.

- Tech solutions are obtained faster.

- Many Cloud vendors do not charge monthly storage fees anymore because these fees do not permit the client the freedom and flexibility to budget for their total yearly fees. Instead, these vendors collect data on the resources the client will need and build a custom server to make sure it is big enough to meet the current needs, but also has lots of room to accommodate growth. This way the client knows the cost of storage and usage for the year and the client can budget and build end user pricing to fit the bill.

Owning Infrastructure

What does it mean to own the infrastructure and should a client own it? Owning infrastructure simply means that the client assumes the responsibilities for purchasing, updating, maintaining, and licensing, to name a few.

When the client doesn't own the infrastructure, the client is not responsible for those items. Working with a responsible Cloud vendor in this situation may be the most workable solution. Bottom lines:

- The Cloud likely is a viable consideration for many businesses or individuals who don't want to own their own infrastructure, especially in situations where it has been shown that significant cost savings will accompany working with a vendor in the Cloud.

- There is a strong and growing movement to operate from co-locations where the risks of having and utilizing hardware and software on the client's site (including lack of redundancy and other security concerns) are reduced if not done away with.

For many, co-locating to the Cloud is reasonable and right. A determination whether or not to co-locate to the Cloud must include additional factors like vendors who use data centers that have the most reliable features available.

Data Centers

It is not uncommon for data centers to have the capability of storing multiple petabytes (PB) of data. This is an astronomical amount of information.

To give this statistic more definition and understanding, one petabyte is equal to one thousand terabytes (TB). One terabyte is equal to one trillion bytes, or 1024 gigabytes (GB). One gigabyte is 1000 megabytes (MB) or one billion bytes, and 1000 kilobytes (KB) equals one megabyte.

Seen another way from smallest to largest:

- 1000 KB = 1 MB

- 1000 MB = 1 GB

- 1000 GB = 1 TB

- 1000 TB = 1 PB

Again, this represents a *lot* of data.

Data centers have certain traits and characteristics which make them almost impervious to loss. A reliable data center will include these provisions:

- Security: this is accomplished in several sequential ways.

Badge identification

Biometric Scan (technology that recognizes actual human beings who physically have to be present for entry in the system)

Codes—unique to each individual

Man Trap (a form of physical security employing two sets of interlocking doors)

Here's an example of use: a badge is required to enter a data center through the first door of two. The first door closes and locks and the second door can be opened only with a biometric scan. If a person seeking entry doesn't pass the biometric technology scan then both doors remain locked and authorities are summoned to investigate what likely could be a breach of security.

- Power rating of 12+ Megawatts: To put this into perspective, one megawatt powers 12,000 houses. A "mega" is a unit for measuring power that is equivalent to one million watts (or one joule per second). It is plain to see that the power capability at a data center is massive.

- Cooling Systems: As long as you can cool it, you can store it.

- Fire Suppression: This includes several components.

One is a set of alarms the employ loud noises and flashing lights as warning systems.

Another is the strategic placement of portable fire extinguishers throughout the data center.

Yet another is locating emergency "power off" switches in plain view.

Finally, all power and data cables are separated.

- Physical Security: In today's world, security *is* the biggest concern. From the moment an individual puts information in the Cloud, security is important and it will remain so.

Data centers should have several physical elements that serve as battering rams and physical protection devices that safeguard an organization's data. One is bullet resistant glass. Certain areas of the data center, especially the entry areas including the lobby, should be protected by bullet proof or bullet resistant glass.

Another is the use of electronic Access Control Systems (ACS): all entry points should have electronic access which only allows access to the data center to authorized individuals. Several types of electronic access systems exist, including biometric safeguards, palm readers, finger printer readers, and security swipe badges.

Handling visitors is another important consideration. All visitors must be properly identified with a current and valid form of identification, and each visitor must be given a temporary facility badge that permits access to certain areas within the data center. This process must be documented in an entry ticketing system.

And no physical security provision would be complete without alarms on all exterior doors and throughout all sensitive areas within the facility. These alarms are hardwired and virtually tamper-free.

And one more: cameras are everywhere. Security cameras should be placed throughout all critical areas, both inside and out of the data center. These cameras are both fixed and PTZ (pan, tilt, zoom). What they see is constantly monitored by highly trained security personnel at multiple locations. They are mounted in many locations throughout five data centers, and all the centers are watching each other.

- Hands-on services: "Hands-on" is a term that means a real person is present to conduct necessary procedures. These procedures often include on-site technical assistance for any hardware systems failures.

  One is visual verification to assist with remote

troubleshooting. There are some tasks human beings' eyes are best qualified to observe.

Also, hands-on services perform removable backups to insure redundancy, physically plugging in a device and then removing the device once the data has been copied over.

Plus, hand-on services address the need of power cycling devices. Sometime devices require a hard boot reset and this action necessitates an individual to go to a cabinet rack and activate the reset power button to physically reset the hardware.

Finally, rack mounted installation and wiring of new equipment are parts of hands-on services. When new servers or hardware are placed into service these devices have to be rack mounted and configured. Human hands do these jobs.

With all of these considerations in place it is more than apparent that choosing the right Cloud vendor is highly important. Reliability is the key to provision and personal customer service.

Vendor Checklist

A Vendor Checklist may be valuable. Here's what a reliable vendor will have and utilize:

- SAS-70 Type II Audit—where a 3rd party has come in and audited the security, protocols, and systems in place.

- Accredited Managed Service Provider—MSP Alliance, another 3rd party certification to ensure proper security, protocols and systems are in place.

- Authorized brand Commercial Host—to ensure the user is not violating user agreements by hosting the application with a non-licensed vendor.

- SLA—Service Level Agreement, to understand what guarantees of uptime your provider is giving you, know who owns the data and what type of backups are being provided.

- Availability Support/Self Service Help Desk—24/7. It's important to understand what resources are given to each user and what is included or costs extra for technical support and training.

- Private Label—if branding your firm is important, then having a service provider that offers white label options should be a question to ask as well as if there are additional fees for this upgrade.

- Storage Fees—these can rack up quickly and turn a $50.00 monthly billing fee into hundreds of dollars per month.

Be sure you understand your storage limitations and any applicable fees. This also goes for memory and bandwidth usage.

- Restriction of Applications—it's important to understand all of your options, to know if you will need to house applications locally or go to another vendor for hosting of certain apps. Many Cloud providers have a small portfolio of what they will host.

- Server Administration—determining your Cloud administrator and, if it's the Cloud provider, knowing what fees are associated with this service.

- License Fees—these can add up from server licenses to application fees and vendor fees. Make sure you understand any ancillary costs.

- Seamless Windows—most accountants work on dual screen monitors so it is important to find out the compatibility and limitations as well as test the functionality before signing up.

The vendor's data center must be nearly impervious to threats and offer protection mechanisms to address negative occurrences. While nothing is absolutely certain in this environment, accessing and working in the Cloud with a reliable vendor is one of the closest and surest options available.

The Opportunity

Opportunities come in all forms, all the time. From the online series entitled *Leadership Initiatives* article, *Recognizing and Seizing Opportunity*: "Opportunity comes. Daily, weekly, minute by minute—it is there. Recognizing and responding to it are easy when times are good. Seizing opportunity and making something of it when times are not good, especially within challenging economic circumstances, can be tough.

"One responsibility of a leader is to uncover opportunity and act upon it. A strong leader views the broad landscape of factors, considers courses, and firmly decides on the basis of principle whether to act on an opportunity, taking the initiative if the answer is 'yes.'

"Positive action overcomes doubt, replaces fear with faith and faithfulness, and generates production. Results can be nothing short of remarkable. One example: the 'what if' of explorative thinking—a necessary part of innovation and strategic planning—becomes a part of the process when opportunity is recognized and action is engaged.

"Too many leaders and followers get caught up in wishing and waiting for far too long. Of course, time and consideration are necessary parts of deciding any proper course. But once opportunity is uncovered and decisions are reached, dedicated action commences. Goals are set, tasks fulfilled.

"This is progress. It's a repeating cycle. Right action produces desired results. Results generate new and expanded opportunities. This process recurs for any who recognize and seize it."

I see working together in the Cloud as a remarkable opportunity. For many taking advantage of this chance for change may be optional at this time. For others, it is incumbent upon them that they move quickly to embrace the Cloud and all it has to offer.

As an accounting professional I have literally seen new technology transform the ways in which business is conducted. Enthusiasm is high and it should be for any IT product that engages people, improves their work environment, and fosters increased production and profit.

What was stated at the outset should be reaffirmed: "The Cloud has forever altered how we store and share information. It improves the way we create, manage, and utilize data vital to business and personal application. The Cloud has changed our computing environment.

"Some people resist change. Others embrace it. Those who adapt to new methodologies learn that it's all about using advanced technologies to help us become better at what we do. It's all about creating and using tools that make positive differences in other people's lives."

I am convinced this is what the Cloud does. Those who are ready for positive change will take advantage of this growth opportunity, for themselves, the companies they serve, and their customers. The benefits will be far reaching.

Acknowledgements

Many people contribute to the success of writing a book and seeing it published. I would like to give special thanks to Kacee Johnson, one of my closest associates, for her advice and encouragement throughout this whole process. Ronald P. Spagnola was one of our editors and has been a supporter of my business efforts for a long time. Thanks to Alexander Paul who contributed to the diagrams. Glen Aubrey and his team at Creative Team Publishing (www.CreativeTeamPublishing. com) contributed their expertise, also editing the manuscript and covering the details of the publishing process.

I also want to acknowledge the accounting and business communities as well as my staff who have recognized me as a leader in Cloud computing. Leaders in any field must be supported by those who follow. Together leaders and followers help make each other successful.

Finally, I want to especially thank my lovely wife, Brianna, who has believed in me throughout my career, and my lovely daughter. They always will be the loves of my life in success or through discouragement. No matter the circumstances, their love is complete and unconditional.

The Author

Robert J. Chandler is an acknowledged industry visionary and leader in Cloud technology. He was honored with the award of "Top 40 Under 40" by the CPA Practice Advisor Magazine in 2007, 2008, and 2010.

He is also a leading national advocate of modern accounting methods that include universal Internet service with remote access to client files, outsourcing of bookkeeping work, automated accounting systems and techniques, professional certification for all bookkeeping practitioners, and Cloud computing advancements for an aging industry.

He is a sought-after speaker for Accounting and Technology conferences nationwide, and is actively involved in moving the accounting industry forward with advancements in technology.

Robert can be contacted through his website: www. RobertJChandler.com and www.togetherinthecloud.com.

CPSIA information can be obtained at www.ICGtesting.com
Printed in the USA
BVOW041923290412

288886BV00002B/2/P